CLINK

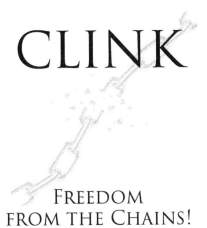

CLINK

FREEDOM
FROM THE CHAINS!

BY DR. BARRY AMACKER

XULON PRESS

Xulon Press
2301 Lucien Way #415
Maitland, FL 32751
407.339.4217
www.xulonpress.com

Unless otherwise indicated, Scripture quotations taken from The King James Version; The New Living Translation (NLT). Copyright © 1996, 2004, 2007 by Tyndale House Publishers, Inc.

Unless otherwise indicated, Scripture quotations taken from The New International Version (NIV). Copyright © 1973, 1978, 1984, 2001 by Biblica, Inc.

Unless otherwise indicated, Scripture quotations taken from The Message (MSG) Copyright © 1993, 1994, 1995, 1996, 2000, 2001, 2002, by NavPress Publishing.

Unless otherwise indicated, Scripture quotations taken from The English Standard Version (ESV) Crossway Good News Publishers.

Unless otherwise indicated, Scripture quotations taken from The American Standard Version (ASV); Amplified Bible (AMP) c 2015 The Lockman Foundation.

Printed in the United States of America.

ISBN-13: 978-1-5456-7242-6

Some sat in darkness and deepest gloom, imprisoned in iron chains of misery. They rebelled against the words of God, scorning the counsel of the Most High. That is why he broke them with hard labor; they fell, and no one was there to help them. Lord, help, they cried in trouble and he saved them from their distress. He led them from the darkness and deepest gloom; he snapped their chains.

Psalms 107:10-14 (NLT)

Dedication

I would like to dedicate this book to my grandchildren Adalyn, Avery, Anderson and any other grandchildren we may be blessed with in the future. They are my "Why." In any endeavor, we have to know our "why" to keep us focused and motivated.

It has been said, "If we have the opportunity to read a book written by a 90 year old person, we should read it." Why would we not want to read in a few hours what it took a person 90 years to realize? While I am not 90 years old (at this time 2019), it is important for me to share this information so others will have some insight that I have gained in my life, so far. I realized in writing this book that Satan's schemes are the same today as they were in Bible days, and I am certain they will continue to be prevalent in the days ahead for my grandchildren, and yours.

Likewise, the Word of God is everlasting, faithful and true. I trust this book will be a caution light for my grandchildren, and all who read it, to avoid wrong turns that will end on dead end streets locked out from the purpose and blessings God has for their lives.

About the Author

B arry Amacker is currently the Superintendent of Education of the Jackson County School District in Mississippi (2019). Previously, he served as a band director, assistant principal, and principal in the Mobile County Public School System in Mobile, Alabama, and as a principal and assistant superintendent in the Jackson County School District in Mississippi.

He was born in Mobile, Alabama, but currently lives in Ocean Springs, Mississippi. After graduation from Moss Point High School, he attended the University of South Alabama and earned a bachelor of science in music education. Later he earned a master's in education from the University of South Alabama, as well as a doctorate in education from Nova Southeastern University.

Along with maintaining his professional career in education, Barry has served as minister of music at various churches throughout the years. He was also a part of the Gospel Four, a gospel group that included his father-in-law and mother-in-law, Chopper and Lois Stevenson; his wife Kathy; and various other musicians. While in the Gospel Four (the original name even though there were more than four members), Barry wrote several songs that were recorded by the group.

Additionally, Dr. Amacker is the author of two other books, *These Old Shoes* and *Power to Press On*.

He was named Superintendent of the Year in 2018 for the state of Mississippi, and represented Mississippi in the National Superintendent of the Year Gala.

Table of Contents

Introduction

For you have been called to live in freedom...
Galatians 5:13 (NLT)

W e have been called to live in freedom, so why do we
allow, or cause, ourselves to become bound by the
perils of this life? When we chain ourselves, effectiveness to
accomplish what God desires to do in our lives is diminished or
terminated. *Clink* represents the sound heard when the chains
holding us back fall off and hit the ground, allowing us to actually live in freedom. In Psalm 107, the people had rebelled
against God's commands and despised His plans. Today is
much like the situation described in Psalms 107. Many sit in
darkness, deep gloom and are imprisoned by chains of misery.
Just as they did, it is our action or lack of action that results
in chains that bind us and hinder us from becoming what God
desires in our life.

This book presents many of the chains found in scriptures
that we tend to put on ourselves. Examples of these chains' effect

on people in Bible days and us today are given. Additionally, each chapter will present keys to unlock these chains.

In Psalms 107, the people cried out to Him and He snapped the chains. John 8:36 declares, he that the Son sets free is free indeed. Hopefully, as you read each chapter and use the keys, you will hear the sound "clink" as the chain falls off.

> *If the Son Therefore shall make you free, ye shall be free indeed.*
>
> John 8:36 (KJV)

When the chains are broken, we become free to accomplish God's plan in our lives. In my book *Power to Press On*, I present the importance of building our physical, mental, emotional and spiritual capacity. I believe that building capacity is vital for our success. However, I have come to realize that having the power to press on is not the same as pressing on. Until we actually press on with the capacity we have built, we haven't done anything. So why don't we DO something with the power we have built to press on? I believe it is due to the chains that we allow to easily beset us that hold us back. Let me say, I believe we are less likely to allow the chains to be placed on us, if we have consistently developed in our physical, mental, emotional and spiritual beings. There will always be attacks to try to hold us back. Satan never gives up.

Satan does not care how much power we have to press on unless we use it to actually DO something. This book attempts to identify some of the common chains the enemy uses to hold us back. It also provides some scriptural basis for snapping the chains so that we can hear the sound of the chains dropping. That "Clink" sound strikes fear in the heart of the enemy.

Chapter 1

Chain of Lies

Deliver my soul, O Lord, from lying lips
and from a deceitful tongue.
Psalms 120:2 (KJV)

T he first chapter of this book is called Chain of Lies because I believe the other chains discussed in the following chapters are birthed in the heart of lies. Proverbs 6:16 lists seven things God hates and three of them are pertaining to lies: a lying tongue, a heart that devises wicked purposes, and a false witness that uttereth lies. Lies and deception are some of Satan's most effective tactics. He is a schemer and a liar. A scheme is a plan and design of a plot to create a particular result. Satan's desired result in our lives is for us to fail and fall short of what God desires to do in our lives resulting ultimately in death.

Satan got right to work with his scheme of putting the chains of lies on God's plan. In Genesis 3:2-4, when Satan approached Eve in the Garden of Eden, the essence of the conversation was not about apples, Adam, or the beautiful garden. It was about death. Satan's lie, "You will not die if you disobey God's command", set the tone for the rest of the Bible and the ages.

Putting on the chains of lies may occur in two ways. First, we can be the one telling the lie. Secondly, we can believe the lie. In either case, there are serious consequences associated with being a party to a lie. No doubt, it is a miserable feeling to be a victim of lies when someone lies about us, or when people believe a lie about us. We have to stand firm in faith on God's truth and remember, *the battle is not ours, it's God's* (2 Chronicles 20:15).

In 1 Kings there is a good example of someone believing a lie that had fatal consequences. The Lord told the prophet one set of instructions and then another prophet came along and gave the first prophet contradicting instructions. The first prophet took the second prophet's instructions over what God had originally told him, and it resulted in him being killed by a lion for his disobedience. Interestingly enough, the prophet who lied was not killed. Two valuable points are noteworthy from this account. First, when God gives us a path and direction, rest assured there will be distractions and naysayers along the way that could get us off course if we listen. But the consequences fall on us. Stand firm, be bold, and stay the course. Secondly, on the flip side, be careful not to be the one giving false information. Our words and influence can get others off course leaving us remorseful and full of regret.

Another lie that is believed to this day by many is the devil's answer to "who moved the stone?" To this day many believe the lie that was told on the day of Jesus' resurrection. In Matthew 28:13, when Mary came to the tomb, she realized the stone had been rolled away by the angel. The guards; however, in fear of their own life, accepted a bribe from the leading priest and were told, "You must say, 'Jesus disciples came during the night while we were sleeping, and they stole his body.' If the governor hears about it, we'll stand up for you so you won't get in trouble." This lie is still told and believed today. As stated earlier, there are consequences for believing a lie. If we can't believe the angel moved the stone, how can we believe Jesus can remove the chains that bind us, and prevent us from being what God has for us to be?

By now we see a pattern of how the devil shows up at major intersections throughout the Bible. He will continue to do that in our lives today. Expect it and be on guard with spiritual preparation.

The devil is deceptive. Throughout the Bible he presented a substitute for the real thing. Not only can we be deceived by mimicry, but we can miss what is actually the real thing. Satan will use slander and lies to make the real thing look as if it is a fake. In Matthew, Chapter 27 the crowd had to choose between Jesus Barabbas and Jesus the Christ. The crowd went for the fake, but in the end, it all worked out. Jesus, the stone that the builder rejected, became the cornerstone.

Even in Revelation Chapter 13, we see a fake Trinity. Satan is the fake for God, the antichrist is the fake for Jesus, and the false prophet is the fake Holy Spirit. There is always a fake that looks like the real thing, and sometimes we miss the real thing. But God is in control.

On a lighter note, something occurred to Kathy and me that demonstrated how easily we can become confused in the environment around us, which results in the inability to determine what's real or fake. Yes, I was the fake! A few summers ago while on vacation we were doing a little shopping. I was wearing one of those casual flowery Hawaiian type shirts and a pair of shorts, flip flops and a hat. I had finished browsing before Kathy, and was standing near the door waiting. Another lady, who was shopping, came up and ran her hand across the front of my shirt, felt the sleeves and looked at the back to see if she liked my shirt. I stood still just wondering what was going on. Then I finally asked the lady if I could help her, and I thought she was going to have a heart attack. As it turns out, she thought I was a mannequin modeling the clothes in the store. I realized that my attire was very similar to the type clothing in the store and I was standing near other mannequins displaying the clothes. When I moved, she realized I was the real deal not a mannequin and she apologized profusely. We all got a big laugh out of it, and I asked if she wanted to buy my shirt. If so, I would make her a great deal. It is easy in certain environments to mistaken the real deal for a substitute, or a substitute for the real deal. We need the Holy Spirit to give us discernment in these instances.

There is always a compelling fake, but sooner or later God's power will demonstrate who is in control. In Exodus Chapters 7-8, Moses used his staff to demonstrate God's power by turning it into a snake, frogs, and blood in the Nile. Each time, Pharaoh's magicians were able to replicate the feat. However, when it got to the little bitty gnats, they couldn't do it. The magicians couldn't make a gnat. The tipping point was when they could not even make a gnat, they told Pharaoh "Surely this is the hand of God." God can turn the smallest circumstances in our lives into great tipping points to reveal His glory and true power. Those around us will have to recognize, as did the magicians, that "surely this is the hand of God." He is the real deal, no fakes.

We have to have our own strategy and tactic to overcome these attacks. The best attack against a lie is the truth. We are delivered from the snare of the fowler. We can release ourselves through reading, knowing God's word, and through effectual fervent prayer. As we filter everything through a keen spiritual awareness, we will see through the plots and snares of the fowler. Spiritual keenness comes by preparing mentally, physically, spiritually and emotionally on a regular basis. Being sharp in every dimension of our lives gives us the edge in seeing through the schemes that are around us. Even if we are not aware of the schemes, God still guides through them like a mine field. He knows. Looking back I can see how he has guided me perfectly through situations I was unaware of at the time. He indeed orders our steps and we have to follow his directions.

When someone tells me they are not experiencing any schemes or plots against them, they are really saying to me that they are spiritually blind. Rest assured, Satan is planning your failure. When we are oblivious to his schemes, he just has his way and then suddenly we are ambushed totally unprepared. We absolutely cannot walk out of our house any day without the belt of truth and a keen spiritual awareness.

In 1 Samuel 28:7, Saul's fatal error was relying on a medium for information. Irrespective of whether the information he received was accurate, or not. The fact that Saul relied on the medium rather than God for information resulted in him being separated from God.

I have heard it said that "right is never wrong, and wrong is never right." However, in the spiritual sense, wrong (or what appears to be wrong from our perception) may be the right thing that needs to happen for God's will to be fulfilled. So when we feel that the lies against us have prevailed, we can trust that God is working His plan, and in due time the good will be revealed to us. It is best to hold our peace and not react to what we believe are lies against us, or being told to us. We do not know for sure what is true, and what is not true. Pray for wisdom to be granted to all involved to the lies being told. If we react based on erroneous information, we can cause bigger problems for ourselves. We have to keep believing and trusting in God, then press on!

> *Keep your tongue from evil and your lips from speaking deceit.*
>
> Psalms 34:13 (ESV)

Slander has always been a weapon of Satan and we must not believe the lies of his slander toward us. His goal is to drive us to despair to the point we believe we are not good enough to move forward in the direction God is calling us to, or that our situation is too bad for Him to help. Often we will disqualify ourselves due to a lack of confidence from believing the lies, slander and doubt that the devil pitches to us. When this happens, we lose out on the vision of how individually we can make a difference in the world around us and the course of history. In fact, Jesus was the stone that the builder rejected.

Take heart, we are not by ourselves. Satan even slanders God and Jesus. In Revelation 12, we see that Satan continues to slander Jesus and God, but there is good news found in Chapter 20. Here we read John's account where he saw an angel carrying a large chain and used the chain to bind Satan so that he could no longer lie, deceive and slander for a 1000 years (more on this later).

> *And I saw an angel come down from heaven,*
> *having the key of the bottomless pit and a*
> *great chain in his hand. And he laid hold on*
> *the dragon, that old serpent, which is the Devil,*
> *and Satan, and bound him for a thousand years.*
> Revelation 20:1 (KJV)

We see there is a chain associated with lies and slander, but it ends up on Satan, the old serpent that started things off with a lie in the Garden of Eden. We should not fall into the traps that entangle us with all of the pitfalls associated with lies. In due time, the truth prevails. It has been said that "lies can cover a multitude of sins, temporarily", but sooner or later, we will hear the sound "Clink" when truth prevails.

> *And the devil that deceived them was cast into the lake of fire and brimstone, where the beast and the false prophet are, and shall be tormented day and night forever and ever.*
> Revelation 20:10 (KJV)

Keys to unlock the Chain of Lies

Pray for the Lord to snap the chain of lies.

Know the truth and it will set you free.

Seek the truth by reading the Bible, Praying, and Godly counsel.

Pray for discernment to avoid being tricked by a lie.

Do not repeat negative comments because they may not be true.

Rely on what God says rather than what others say.

Don't accept the lies of the enemy about you. Press on.

Relax knowing that in due time God will reveal the truth and straighten the crooked path.

Be aware of the schemes of the Devil.

Be aware of the fake versus the real thing. The Devil always has a knock off version.

Do not lie or bear false witness.

Chapter 2

Chain of Unforgiveness

And whenever you stand praying, forgive, if you have any-
thing against anyone, so that your Father also who is in
heaven may forgive you your trespasses.
Mark 11:25 (ESV)

In Matthew 18, Jesus speaks a parable of a servant who owed a sum of money to the king. When he was called before the king he begged for more time to fulfill his obligation and the king granted his request. Later, this same servant was owed money by a fellow servant who asked him for more time to fulfill his obligation, but the servant who was owed money refused and locked him up until he could pay every penny. The king heard what had happened and sent for the servant he had granted more time. He had him put in prison and tortured until every penny he owed was paid.

This parable clearly shows how the process of forgiveness works. If we are going to be forgiven, we have to first forgive.

The Lord's Prayer serves as a model on how we should pray, and it says "forgive us our trespasses as we forgive those who trespass against us." Jesus tells us to ask, and receive forgiveness and in turn forgive others who have done things against us. God desires to bless us and restore us, but it is our move. Our failure to forgive, and pray for those who despitefully use us, blocks our own blessing.

Jesus gave a warning in Matthew 7:3-5 about worrying about the speck of sawdust in someone else's eye while having a plank in our own eye. He says, "You hypocrite, first take the plank out of your own eye, and then you will see clearly to remove the speck from your brother's eye."

Honestly, the Holy Spirit has convicted me for looking back on hurtful situations and conjuring up negative feelings about the people and circumstances involved. I have been guilty of this even in situations where God delivered me and I came out victorious. In some cases, looking back is due to my disbelief that someone could do such a hurtful thing. When I do this, I am blocking my own blessing that God desires to send my way.

One good Biblical example of this principle is found in the case of Job. Job was tried and tested by Satan to the point of losing his family and his belongings. During this time of testing, he was mocked and criticized by his "friends", but Job remained faithful. At the end of the story an interesting thing happened. In Job 42:10, God restored all that Job had lost with a double portion AFTER he prayed for his friends who had criticized and discouraged him. This is a wonderful demonstration of letting go of ill feelings, and hurtful things that people do to us. It beckons the question, would the Lord have restored Job if he had not prayed for his friends?

In addition to the spiritual downfall of unforgiveness, physical implications exist. I have known people to hold a grudge against someone for so long they could not even remember why. Often, the other person didn't even know of the grudge and was going happily along their way, while the person holding the grudge was feeling badly due to bitterness that had developed over time. Proverbs 17:22 says, *A merry heart doeth good like a medicine: but a bitter spirit drieth up the bones*. There is an abundance of research that shows the negative impact bitterness can have on our health. Numerous studies confirm that negative emotions are associated with the increased risk of coronary artery disease, heart attack and sudden cardiac death. Conversely, studies have shown that people showing positive emotions were significantly less likely to suffer from heart disease.

So, when we forgive someone, we are releasing ourselves from the ills of the wrongs done to us. If we do not forgive them, we are empowering the wrong done to us exponentially. Forgiveness does not remove the consequence of the wrong done, it removes the negative impact on us mentally, physically, emotionally, and spiritually. In our lives from time to time we need forgiveness and likewise, we have to forgive those who have hurt us. The Lord's Prayer, that we recite often, says "forgive us our debts as we forgive our debtors."

*For with the judgment you pronounce you will
be judged, and with the measure you use it will
be measured unto you.*

Matthew 7:2 (ESV)

We will be judged by the same standard we judge others.
If we set a standard of unforgiveness, not only will we not
be forgiven by others, but we will not be able to forgive ourselves. We have to forgive our self in order to proceed in liberty
and freedom of God's grace. We cannot hold on to ills of the
past and move forward at the same time. Satan will constantly
remind us of our failures and make us feel unworthy to press
on in what God calls us to do. In the scriptures we find many
people in the Bible who had faults and were used mightily. We
too, have to remove the chain of unforgiveness toward others
and ourselves and press on.

To completely fulfill the process of forgiveness, we have
to forgive with our total being, mentally, physically, spiritually
and emotionally (head, heart, and gut). Sometimes we can mentally decide to forgive, and emotionally heal from the hurt, but
until we act on the decision to forgive, it is not complete. John
3:16 declares that God so loved the world that he gave his only
son that we might have everlasting life. God acted on his forgiveness, he didn't think about it, or want to, he gave.

What action can we take that demonstrates we have forgiven individuals for wrongs done to us from the past? Every
situation is different and there is no one thing to define it, but

to completely unlock the chain of un-forgiveness, we have to actually turn the key.

> *Be kind to one another, tenderhearted, forgiving*
> *one another, as God in Christ forgave you.*
> Ephesians 4:32 (ESV)

And then there is the part of accepting forgiveness. When someone asks for our forgiveness the responsibility shifts to us. In Genesis Chapters 32-33, when Jacob was in the process of making peace with Esau, he brought gifts to demonstrate his sincerity. At first, Esau would not accept the gifts, but after Jacob insisted, Esau accepted the gifts. It is difficult sometimes to accept a gift of kindness, and I am guilty of saying, "No thank you, I have plenty." However, the actual gift is not the point, it is the act of giving and allowing the other person to free themselves from the chain and unblock the blessings headed their way.

Kathy and I were at a conference in Savannah, Georgia a few years ago. We squeezed out a little time for a sightseeing tour. During the tour, the narrator pointed out that several of the doors in the historic district were painted red. He shared the fact that it was a tradition to paint the door of a house red when it was paid for. Well, my spiritual thought process kicked in and I thought of the Pass Over, and how the red blood of Jesus redeems us. And that we are paid for with the price of His blood. Jesus stands at the door and knocks, ready to forgive us of our sins. When we open this door and accept his forgiveness of our sins, we have removed the chain of sin and death that unforgiveness brings. In Revelation 3:20, Jesus is standing at the door of the Laodicean church wanting to come in. This could only happen if the people repented. He desires to have fellowship, intimacy, and communion with us. When we open the door, Revelation 19:9 declares we will dine with Christ at the marriage supper of the Lamb and in the millennial kingdom.

> *Behold, I stand at the door, and knock: if any man*
> *hear my voice, and open the door, I will come in*
> *to him, and will sup with him, and he with me.*
> Revelation 3:20 (KJV)

Jesus is standing at the door saying he forgives us, but we have to open the door to allow him to come in. Accepting the mental knowledge of his forgiveness is the beginning, but it is not complete until we act on it and unlock the chain on the door.

Keys to unlock the Chain of Unforgiveness

- Pray for the Lord to snap the chain of unforgiveness.

- Forgive with your total being (physically, mentally, emotionally and spiritually).

- To completely fulfill the forgiveness process, actually do something that demonstrates it.

- Get the plank out of your eye, before criticizing the speck in someone else's eye.

- Forgive others of their trespasses as you would like to be forgiven.

- Pray for those who have hurt you. Job was blessed after he prayed for his accusers.

- Free yourself from the wrongs done to you.

- Accept forgiveness from others when you have wronged them.

Chapter 3

Chain of Fear

And deliver them who through fear of death
were all their lifetime subject to bondage.
Hebrews 2:15 (KJV)

F rom my youngest days I can remember being afraid. In general, fear is a normal reaction to the unknown. Even as adults, we face unexpected things that arise suddenly resulting in fearful reactions. Inherently, we have an intuitive trigger that comes from our instincts to react to dangerous situations that could save our lives. Fear is an emotional outlet that is needed for us to live a healthy balanced life.

Recently, Kathy and I found ourselves in uncharted waters. We live in Ocean Springs, Mississippi, and occasionally have the opportunity take a boat out on the water in the Gulf of Mexico. One afternoon we got brave and decided to follow the channel markers out to Horn Island that is about 12 miles off of the coast. We had never been there, so we were a little anxious. After we were a good distance out, and I am already feeling lost, suddenly the Coast Guard came out of nowhere with flashing lights and someone on the speaker inquiring, "Do you have any weapons on board?"

I thought to myself, "Really, I only have a .22 rifle at home that I have shot 3 times in my whole life and missed the target all three times." Let me say fear showed up in the boat that afternoon. They asked permission to come aboard, and I am thinking, "Have I gone to Mexico?" We soon realized they were conducting a routine general safety inspection. The lesson here is that even though fear can rise up suddenly, often things are not as bad as they seem to be at first. If we remain calm and allow time for faith to overcome fear, things will work out. After this episode, Kathy and I went on and enjoyed a beautiful afternoon on the water.

When we face fearful situations, we need to let the light of Jesus illuminate our path. Then we are not in the dark and can see we are holding the hand of the one who sees and knows all. In our boat ride that afternoon, we were branching out beyond our comfort zone. We do not need to allow fear to hold us back from pursuing uncharted waters in the purpose God has for our lives. If we press on, the Lord will guide us and things will work out. David, in Psalms 34:4 declares, *"I sought the Lord, and he answered me and delivered me from all my fears."*

The fear discussed in this chapter goes beyond the spontaneous reaction to an event or a scary situation to look at fear as a state of being, or a disposition of our character. When we live in a state of fear and allow all of the noise of the enemy to take root, we are paralyzed from accomplishing what God's purpose is for our lives. Leviticus 26:36 speaks of people who become so fearful that the sound of a windblown leaf causes them to run even though no one is actually chasing them.

In contrast, when faced with adversity, we need to see things through our spiritual eyes and perceive what God is doing behind the scenes. When Elisha was being chased by the Syrian King's army, it appeared to Elisha's servant that they were surrounded facing sure defeat. But when Elisha looked out he saw, through his spiritual eyes, the army of the Lord encamped about the whole situation. Elisha prayed for the spirit to open the servant's eyes that he may see, and indeed, he saw that the mountain was full of horses and chariots of fire all around Elisha.

As Christians, we are vulnerable to effects of fear if we walk around oblivious to the fact that God is working on our behalf behind the scenes. He will warn us through our highly engaged spiritual capacity in order that we can prepare ourselves and stand firm with him through the adversity. Additionally, how we respond to adversity speaks loudly to our faith in God. We don't have to run and hide every time the devil says BOO!! If we will say BOO back, under the authority of Jesus' name and the power of the Holy Spirit, he will run. When our TESTimony is tested, we have the opportunity to demonstrate God's power through our lives and radiate an air of confidence to those around us. Conversely, if we panic and come unraveled, we radiate a spirit of fear, rather than a sound mind.

For God hath not given us the spirit of fear; but
of power, and of love, and of a sound mind.

2 Timothy 1:7 (KJV)

I believe, and research shows, that our spirit (heart) impacts the condition of other's hearts with whom we are in close proximity. What do people around us hear? Do they hear the sound "clink" as the chain of fear falls off, or do they hear the rattling sound of the chain of fear being drug around as we run and hide? When we live and move in His name, we will radiate an air of confidence for those around us, which is pleasing to God. When we walk in a room, it should change the atmosphere because of the presence we bring with faith and confidence that God dwells in us. God's power should be the prevailing influence when we are present. Have you ever walked in the woods and noticed that everything changes just by your presence? The animals stop and watch, or run off, or the birds fly to another tree.

Recently, I was doing my physical capacity building at the river by doing a two mile walk down our road to the river house. It is a normal routine for me on days when we stay there. While walking, I listen to the Bible readings for that day, pray, and meditate amongst the beautiful scenery. I have developed a pretty good understanding with the dogs down that road. They are used to seeing me come by, and getting a little pat from me. However, on this particular day, there was a pit bull I had never seen before that started running toward me in a very aggressive manner. I managed to remain calm and continued walking at my normal pace. To my amazement, when this aggressive pit bull got just a few yards away, he stopped cold in his tracks, put his head on the ground, and began to slowly drag himself closer to me. When he got up to me (this probably was not smart), I reached down and patted his head before I walked on by. I reflected on this situation later and wondered what could have caused the dog's reaction. Was it my ability to remain calm and radiate a spirit of confidence and a sound mind? Did the pit bull see something in the spirit realm, like my guardian angel? (Remember Balaam's donkey that saw the angel that Balaam didn't see? –Numbers 22:21) There are a couple of the little bitty dogs that still cut up when I walk by, and I am praying that the Lord will open their spiritual eyes soon and allow them to see whatever the pit bull saw.

> *Have I not commanded thee? Be strong and of a good courage; be not afraid, neither be thou dismayed: for the Lord thy God is with thee whithersoever thou goest.*
>
> Joshua 1:9 (KJV)

One thing is for certain, our very presence can bring a change into a place or situation. If we are moving in God's will, we can be a conduit for His power to be revealed through us, then and there. No matter how small or insignificant we may feel, everything we do speaks. The Bible tells us that when we have done all to stand, then just stand. In 1 Kings 19, Elijah was in a state of fear and discouragement (more on this later) and the Lord instructed him to go stand on the mountain. When he did, a mighty windstorm came, followed by an earthquake and finally a fire. So what happens if Elijah does not go stand on the mountain? What happens if we don't face our fears?

Everything we do and say, or fail to do, impacts things around us and has an exponential effect. In chaos theory, the *butterfly effect* is the sensitive dependence on initial conditions in which a small change in one state of a deterministic nonlinear system can result in large differences in a later state. Edward Lorenz, an American mathematician, meteorologist, and pioneer of chaos theory, coined the term *butterfly effect* from the metaphorical example that the path of a tornado can be influenced by minor perturbations such as the flapping of the wings of a distant butterfly several weeks earlier. What will our perturbations contribute to the environment around us? Will we be flapping around spreading fear, or faith?

Polycarp is one of Christendom's most famous martyrs. He had been a Christian his whole life, and caused quite a stir. For some reason the Romans decided at age 86, they had had enough of his resistance. The 86 year old bishop of Smyrna overcame fear and refused to recant his faith. As a result, the decision was made to burn him at the stake. Soldiers then grabbed him to nail him to a stake, but he stopped them and said, "Leave me as I am. For he who grants me to endure the fire will enable me also to remain on the pyre unmoved, without the security of nails." He drew strength from a voice from heaven saying, "Be strong Polycarp, play the man." Witnesses to this martyrdom reported that as Polycarp was burned, the aroma released in the atmosphere (butterfly effect) was not of burning flesh, but a sweet aroma as bread baking or as gold and silver refined in a furnace. Further, they reported that Polycarp's death was remembered by everyone. It is the first recorded martyrdom in post-New Testament church history. The butterfly effect he released that day is still causing perturbations today by all who hear the story, even in this book. Hopefully, it will move us to proceed with faith and trust in God and strive to fulfill God's purpose in our lives. What will your butterfly effect be?

> *Be of good courage, and let us play the man for*
> *our people, and for the cities of our God: and*
> *the Lord do that which seemeth him good.*
> 2 Samuel 10:12 (KJV)

Fear ends where faith begins. Hebrew 11:6 tells us that it is impossible to please God without faith. It is not that God is pleased because we have faith, but He is pleased with action we take that is founded on our faith. Additionally, James 2:26 states, *Faith without works is dead.* God puts many of our greatest blessings on the other side of fear. We have to press on with faith in order to claim those blessings. Psalms 23:4 tells us that even though we walk through the valley of the shadow of death, not to fear evil because He is with us and protects us. Then in verse 5, we see the table set before us, on the other side of the valley of the shadow of death. We see here, if we press on through despite fear of the shadow of death, we make it to the blessing of the table that is set for us on the other side of our fear.

Yea, though I walk through the valley of the shadow of death, I will fear no evil: for thy rod and thy staff they comfort me. Thou pre-parest a table before me in the presence of my enemies: thou annointest my head with oil; my cup runneth over.

Psalms 23:4-5 (KJV)

Throughout the Bible there are examples of individuals facing fear with faith. Hebrews Chapter 11 is often referred to as the Hall of Fame of Faith. All of these people earned a good reputation because of their faith.

Abel offered unto God a more excellent sacrifice than Cain.

Enoch was taken up to Heaven without dying.

Noah built a large boat for safety from the flood.

Abraham obeyed God's call to leave home for another land.

Sarah was able to have a child at an old age.

Abraham offered Isaac as a sacrifice.

Isaac promised blessings to his sons.

Joseph confidently proclaimed the people of Israel would leave Egypt.

Moses' parents disobeyed the king's demand by hiding Moses for 3 months.

Moses chose to share the oppression of God's people rather than stay in Egypt.

People of Israel went right through the Red Sea on dry ground.

People of Israel marched 7 times around Jericho and the walls fell.

Rahab was not destroyed for giving a friendly welcome to the spies.

Gideon, Barak, Samson, Jephthah, David, Samuel, and all of the prophets are included.

Shadrach, Meshach and Abednego were bound and thrown in a fiery furnace refusing to bow down to king Nebuchadnezzar's image, but they stood firm in their faith and were delivered. Daniel was thrown in the lions' den for standing firm in his prayer life.

In each of these cases their faith did not remove the problem, but it did remove the fear. In the end, they were delivered and elevated to a higher position than before. Rest assured we will end up in the lion's den or the fiery furnace of sorts when we pursue God's purpose in our lives. We have to face our fears with courage knowing that fear produces bondage, but faith produces liberty. When that liberty comes, we can hear the sound "Clink" if we listen through our spiritual ears.

> *For ye have not received the spirit of bondage*
> *again to fear; but ye have received the Spirit of*
> *adoption, whereby we cry, Abba, Father.*
> Romans 8:15 (KJV)

Keys to unlock the Chain of Fear

Pray for the Lord to snap the chain of fear.

Have faith.

Do not allow your imagination to run away with "what if" thoughts.

Write in a journal and reflect on victories of the past.

Trust that God will come through for you.

Do not rely on what you see, but rather what God's word says.

Refrain from verbalizing your fear that gives the Devil encouragement.

Refrain from verbalizing your fear that informs your system to react negatively.

Refrain from verbalizing your fear that weakens your testimony about your faith in God.

Chapter 4

Chain of Addiction

No temptation has overtaken you that is not common to man.
God is faithful, and he will not let you be tempted beyond
your ability, but with the temptation he will also provide the
way of escape, that you may be able to endure it.
The devil, for the devil has been sinning from the beginning.
The reason the Son of God appeared was to destroy
the works of the devil.
1 Corinthians 10:13 (ESV)

Addiction is the state of being enslaved to a habit or practice or to something that is psychologically or physically habit forming as narcotics, to such an extent that its cessation causes severe trauma. It is further defined as the compulsive and uncontrollable use of drugs despite the adverse consequences. Dependence occurs when the body adapts to the presence of a drug, causing withdrawal symptoms when drug use is reduced or discontinued.

According to a United Kingdom charity, Action on Addiction, one in three people in the world have an addiction of some kind. Addiction can come in the form of dependence of any substance or behavior. The most well-known and serious addictions are to drugs and alcohol. Nearly 1 in 10 Americans have an addiction to both. Of the people with a drug addiction, more than two-thirds also abuse alcohol. The most common drug addictions are nicotine, THC, and cocaine. Additionally, According to the National Institute on Drug Abuse and the Centers for Disease Control, the U.S. is in the midst of an opioid epidemic.

There were approximately 20.6 million people in the United States over the age of 12 with an addiction in 2011. According to the National Institute on Drug Abuse and the National Survey on Drug Use and Health, over 3 million people in 2011 received treatment for their addiction.

* Over 20 million Americans over the age of 12 have an addiction (excluding tobacco).
* 100 people die every day from drug overdoses. This rate has tripled in the past 20 years.
* Over 5 million emergency room visits in 2011 were drug related.
* 2.6 million people with addictions have a dependence on both alcohol and illicit drugs.
* 9.4 million people in 2011 reported driving under the influence of illicit drugs.

*   6.8 million people with an addiction have a mental illness.

*   Rates of illicit drug use are highest among those aged 18 to 25.

*   Over 90% of those with an addiction began drinking, smoking or using illicit drugs before the age of 18.

Besides nicotine, drugs and alcohol, there are behaviors that can trigger addiction. Gambling, anger, food, technology, sex and work can become addictive behaviors, to mention a few. In the case of an addiction, a person will typically react negatively when they don't get their "reward." For example, someone addicted to coffee can experience physical and psychological withdrawal symptoms such as severe headaches and irritability.

> *So get rid of all evil behavior. Be done with all deceit, hypocrisy, jealousy, and unkind speech. Like newborn babies, you must crave pure spiritual milk so that you will grow into a full experience of salvation. Cry out for this nourishment...*
> 1 Peter 2:1-2 (NLT)

The chain of addiction can bind us mentally, physically, emotionally and spiritually. In my book Power to Press On, I stress the importance of having air in all four of those tires to be able to roll effectively. The best plan to overcome addiction is to not become addicted in the first place. The old adage "an ounce of prevention is better than a pound of cure" is fitting when it comes to addiction. If we do things daily to put air in each of the four tires, we will be prepared to stand when the enemy comes in like a flood with pressure and temptation.

> *Submit yourselves, then, to God. Resist the devil,*
> *and he will flee from you.*
>
> James 4:7 (ESV)

How do people become addicted? In some cases, it begins with trying to escape, even briefly, from the pressures of life and grows from there as one thing leads to another. Sometimes it is an attempt to fulfill an emptiness or longing of their heart. Other times, as a result of peer pressure and the desire to be accepted, people go along with the crowd and get involved in addictive behaviors. Other times, it can be a reaction to compulsive behaviors out of control. But whatever the case, the devil knows our weaknesses and will attack us where we are most vulnerable.

> *...but each person is tempted when they are*
> *dragged away by their own evil desire and*
> *enticed. Then, after desire has conceived, it*
> *gives birth to sin; and sin, when it is full grown*
> *gives birth to death.*
>
> James 1: 14-15 (ASV)

So how do we *resist* the Devil? First and foremost, we should rebuke the devil through the power of the Holy Spirit and the authority of Jesus' name. When we do this, God will help us. Notice I said "help us" and that means we have to do something for Him to help us with. As we take steps to resist the devil with our head brain (mental capacity), heart brain (emotional and spiritual capacities) and gut brain (physical capacity), He will help us. As discussed earlier, the more we have prepared and developed in each of our capacities, the more likely we are to overcome temptation when the enemy comes in like a flood. However, if we have not prepared and do not have all of our capacities functioning at a high level, it will be difficult. Once we yield to temptation, we risk becoming a slave to our sin and put on the chains that hold us back from what God's purpose is for our lives.

Jesus himself was tempted, as recorded in Matthew, Mark, and Luke. In dealing with attacks of temptation, Jesus did not focus on the temptation; he rebuked Satan with the word. There is a difference between rebuking Satan and resisting temptation. It has been said that whatever we resist, persists. Satan tempting Jesus with bread while he was fasting is a good example of how he attacks us on our weaknesses. Jesus couldn't deny that He was hungry. He had to acknowledge He was hungry. Then he changed the focus back to rebuking the devil rather than having to resist that natural desire for food.

Likewise, when we are tempted, we should pause and use our mental capacity (head brain) to ask, "What do I really need?" Then acknowledge the need, but respond from our core values, rather than impulse. Satan is trying to distract us from our real purpose in life. One key thing to assist in this process is to build time between the stimulus and our response. One technique is to pause and engage in a deep breathing exercise (6 seconds in and 6 seconds out- repeat several times) to allow our emotional capacity and spiritual capacity (heart brain) time to embrace the need and react with our inner core values, and beliefs, to rebuke the devil. Research has shown that breathing and swallowing engage our total being and helps to synergize our head, heart, and gut. To simply try to resist the compulsion, without a process, will lead to a further and more intense persistent draw toward the temptation. We will never convince ourselves we are not hungry, so acknowledge the hunger and change the focus to rebuking the devil. Relying on our own willpower is a dangerous path. Low willpower gives greater focus to the things trying to be resisted, and spirals us downward until willpower collapses completely and desire overcomes our actions. When our willpower collapses one time, it is easier for it to collapse the next time, and the next...

Once again, the more we have our inner being prepared mentally, physically, emotionally, and spiritually, the more likely we will have a synergetic state existing in our being that possesses the capacity to respond effectively. 2 Timothy 1:6 tells us to *fan the spiritual flame the gift of God, which is in you*. Here, the spirit denotes our human spirit, regenerated and indwelt by the Holy Spirit. Rather than relying on things of this world to fill the desires and longing of our spirit, we should fill it with the spiritual flame of God. When we allow the Holy Spirit to fill that longing, He will destroy the yoke.

*There is a path before each person that seems
right, but it ends in death.*
Proverbs 14:12 (NLT)

No one is immune from falling into temptation, but when those times come, there is good news. There is hope through our Lord Jesus Christ. God did his greatest work for the people while they were in the desert. When we are on the bottom and there appears to be no hope, God's grace is sufficient in every situation.

*But he said to me, "My grace is sufficient for
you, for my power is made perfect in weakness."*
2 Corinthians 12:9 (ESV)

A friend of mine, a great community leader in Jackson County Mississippi, was a victim of alcohol addiction. It destroyed his life and he nearly died.

Here is his story in his own words. (Used with permission)

> I hadn't slept or eaten in days and the freezing rain
> was coming at me sideways. I was soaked from
> head to toe. I remember thinking I was going to
> freeze to death, but I had to keep moving as I
> was in a horrible part of town in New Orleans.
> I staggered to get to this bank on Broad Street
> where it was well lit and had this overhang that
> would protect me from the elements, as well as,
> from the thugs that roamed the streets. It was

Monday night, December 7, 1998 around 11pm. I collapsed under the ATM machine and took a sip from the bottle of rubbing alcohol I had in my pocket. I was crying as I passed out... Today is 20 years later and I have never had to take another drink. Life is just a tad better. In fact, the last time I checked, life is pretty darn good.

** Listen everyone to what I am about to say ** Don't ever give up...WITH GOD, ALL THINGS ARE POSSIBLE !!!!!

The rest of the story is that Todd became a successful business man and a community leader that helps raise millions of dollars to help people in need and organizations throughout the area. To God be the Glory.

Todd participated in The Home of Grace, a program in our area that had wonderful success in helping him recover from substance abuse addictions. The Home of Grace, not only has a good program, but it also has a spiritual component that I believe is the crucial component in overcoming addictions. How else can we fill the longing that drove us to the addiction in the first place, if not with the spiritual comfort that the Holy Spirit brings? Just as it is with our small children, when we take something away that they shouldn't be playing with, they cry. If we replace it with something better, they are more content. Just as Todd did, those struggling with addiction should seek professional and spiritual help.

On the day of Pentecost, when the crowd proclaimed, "They're just drunk, that's all." Peter told them these people are not drunk as you suppose. Instead you are seeing what was predicted long ago by the prophet Joel, when he declared, in the last days God would pour out His spirit on all people.

> *And be not drunk with wine, wherein is excess,*
> *but be filled with the Spirit.*
> Ephesians 5:18 (KJV)

As you arrive at the Home of Grace, referred to earlier, you drive through a beautiful area and a winding road with a serene setting. The road winds around and when you get to the very end of the road, there is a beautiful chapel with a cross. The men's choir, made up of participants at the Home of Grace, sing a song written especially for this chapel at the end the end of the road. The lyrics refer to "finding grace at that place at the end of the road." This song touches me every time I hear the guys sing because I realize that it is more than idle words to them. These guys got to the end of the road that drugs and alcohol took them to, but at the end of the road, the cross was waiting to pick them up with a brand new start.

> *And it shall come to pass in that day, that his*
> *burden shall be taken away from off thy shoulder,*
> *and his yoke shall be destroyed because of the*
> *anointing.*
> Isaiah 10:27 (KJV)

Keys to unlock the Chain of Addiction

🔑 Pray for the Lord to snap the chain of addiction.

🔑 Seek professional help.

🔑 Remember an ounce of prevention is better than a pound of cure.

🔑 Avoid situations where you can be tempted through peer pressure to experiment with recreational use of harmful things.

🔑 Build a strong core value system and inner strength by developing mentally, physically, spiritually, and emotionally every day.

🔑 Acknowledge the temptation, but respond with your highly developed inner strength.

🔑 Keep a daily journal to build your faith and record your struggles and victories over temptation.

🔑 Develop relationships with individuals who are not likely to lure you into tempting situations.

🔑 Hunger and thirst after righteousness.

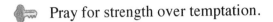 Pray for strength over temptation.

Fan the spiritual flame.

Chapter 5

Chain of the Past

Brothers, I do not consider that I have made it on my own.
But one thing I do: forgetting what lies behind and straining
forward to what lies ahead, I press on toward the goal for the
prize of the upward call of God in Christ Jesus.
Philippians 3:13-14(ESV)

O ur past absolutely matters. Malcolm Gladwell, in his book *Outliers*, shares data that indicates where and when we are born and who our parents are impacts our path in life. These factors, and more, have an impact on success in school, career paths, mortality rate, and health. In fact, throughout the Bible many times when individuals are mentioned by name, it is also stated who this person is the son or daughter of. In the Bible (1 Samuel 16) after Samuel had anointed David to become king, Saul asked David whose son he was. He responded with these historically powerful words, "His name is Jesse, and we live in Bethlehem." When we are born our impact on this life begins and we get in step with what God plans for our life. Our job is to stay in step. It is not a linear path from point A to point B. As in the case of David, there were a lot of ups and downs, successes and failures. However, through it all, David preserved the lineage of Jesus and that changed everything!!

Things from our past impact our present condition. As we make decisions and create our thoughts for the future, our being as it exists now, based on all of our experiences of the past, come to bare. However, we have to make the choice to create the thoughts concerning our past in a positive way. Even though there may have been negative things of the past, we can choose to create positive thoughts about them. For example, our thoughts could be, "I learned from my mistakes and now I am doing better in that situation." By doing this, we avoid wallowing in all of the negative things all over again.

One way to put our past in perspective is to write in a journal. I am a big proponent of keeping a journal because it affords me the opportunity to look back and see how God has seen me through situations of the past, and allows me to learn from my mistakes. Additionally, it is a record for my future generations to know of my journey.

Drawing from the past of others can save us a great deal of misery and regrets. It has been said, "If you have the opportunity to read a book by a 90 year old man, you can save yourself a lot time by knowing what he already figured out." I am so thankful my mom kept a journal, and my dad had kept good notes. When reading these, I get a perspective on life that I would not have understood at the time had my parents merely told me about it. But writing it down, preserved it for me to understand now that I am older.

> *This shall be written for the generation to come:*
> *and the people which shall be created shall*
> *praise the LORD.*
>
> Psalms 102:18 (KJV)

Satan would have us to dwell on our mistakes and failures to distract us from the future plans God has for our lives. I believe that our past can either be a chain to hold us back, or a firm foundation on which to stand as we take our next steps. Our past becomes a chain when we allow Satan to use it as a source of condemnation, to make us feel as if we have no value and can't forgive ourselves. If he can make us feel as if we have no value because of our past, he does not have to defeat us because we defeat ourselves by putting the chain on ourselves. But we do have value. The fact of the matter is that old crinkled up 100 dollar bill still has value.

"The Enemy wants to define you by your scars. Jesus wants to define you by His" –Louie Giglio.

Of course there are those that are quick to judge us for our past, but Jesus put that notion in proper perspective in the way he dealt with the woman caught in adultery. In John 8:1-8, a crowd gathered including religious leaders and the Pharisees.

They pressed Jesus to judge her, but he turned the table and began to write in the sand. He said, "All right, but let the one who has never sinned throw the first stone." One by one they slipped away. Jesus asked her, "Where are your accusers? Didn't even one of them condemn you?" She replied, "No Lord." Jesus replied to her saying, "Neither do I, go and sin no more."

> *There is therefore now no condemnation to them which are in Christ Jesus, who walk not after the flesh, but after the Spirit.*
>
> Romans 8:1 (KJV)

We have to forgive ourselves of negative things and mistakes of the past. It has been said, "Don't cling to a mistake just because you spent a lot of time making it." We should speak and think on things as we expect them to be rather than the way they appear to be. We determine the environment we live in based on the words we speak, whether positive or negative. We are new creatures in Christ Jesus. We have to move on and not track yesterday's mud into today's environment.

> *Therefore, if any man be in Christ, he is a new creature: old things are passed away; behold, all things are become new.*
>
> 2 Corinthians 5:17 (KJV)

Recently, Kathy and I went to see our grandchildren to celebrate Avery's, our second granddaughter, 5th birthday. However, we had to go a week early because of a conflict for the week of her actual birthday. We got there to spend a special day just for her to do whatever she wanted to do. When her day started, I asked her if it was okay if we celebrated her birthday early. She said, "Yes Papa because I already feel 5 anyway." Oh my, "from the mouths of babes" is such a true statement. Live by faith not by sight. Through the blood of Jesus and our faith in him we can already feel 5, redeemed, and live in that environment.

For we walk by faith, not by sight.
2 Corinthians 5:7 (KJV)

There was a lady about to have a baby (1 Samuel 4) during the time when the Ark of the Covenant had been stolen. She named her baby Ichabod which means, the spirit of the lord has departed. She chose to memorialize this negative event by naming her baby in remembrance of the event. She could have just as easily given the baby a name that represented the notion, the spirit of the lord shall return; which it did in a future time. We should give our future expectations a positive result rather than the present negative result. Avery could have said, "But I am only four." Instead she said, "I already feel 5."

When looking at other people who may already feel five, we need to allow them to let go of their past too. As stated earlier, we have to forgive ourselves, but we also need to allow others to forgive themselves.

*And be not conformed to this world: but be ye
transformed by the renewing of your mind, that
ye may prove what is that good, and acceptable,
and perfect will of God.*

Romans 12:2 (KJV)

Another way the past can chain us is by being bound to tradition. It has been said that the only thing more powerful than God's word is our religious traditions. We have to be willing to let God do a new thing in our lives, and not limit Him to our old ways of thinking and doing. Throughout the Bible there was the struggle between the people's attachment to The Law versus God's gift of grace, through Christ Jesus. The world changes and we have to respond to the changes in order to be effective. Just because we have always done something a particular way does not mean it has to continue. We can miss wonderful opportunities God is sending our way, if we are narrow minded rather than being opened minded and allowing God's creativity to work through us for such a time as this. In Luke 5:37-39, Jesus, in a parable regarding new wine placed in old wine skins, indicates he has brought something new and the rituals, and traditions of official Judaism cannot contain it. He acknowledges that it will not be easy by saying the old wine is good, so people will not want to try the new.

*And no one puts new wine in old into old wine-
skins; otherwise the new wine will burst the skins*

and will be spilled out, and the skins ruined. But
new wine must be put into fresh wineskins.
Luke 5:37-38 (AMP)

We do not, however, want to ignore positive benefits of the past that can help us. Sometimes we have to reflect on the victories of the past to guide us through those periods of fear and a lack of faith that come our way during difficult times. David had seriously been betrayed by Saul due to a jealous spirit. David remained loyal through it all. David was running in fear from Saul who was in pursuit of him in an attempt to kill him (1 Samuel 21). David fled to the tabernacle in Nob and Ahimelech, the priest greeted him. Since he left in haste, he did not have any food or a weapon. David inquired of him, "Do you have a weapon?" Being that this was a camp for only the priest, there were no weapons with the exception of one. The priest revealed, wrapped in a cloth in a chest behind the ephod in the temple, one sword. It was the sword of Goliath that was laid up as a monument of the glorious victory David had over him. David, reflecting on the great victory of the past over Goliath and recognizing that it was God's power that brought victory that day, said, "Ah, there is none like this one." David's faith was strengthened and he escaped from Saul.

Truly, there is none like the sword of God's word. Recently, I was going through a tough time in my professional life. Over a several month period, I was in a situation in which I felt betrayed, lied about and misrepresented. But as it turned out, while we were still cleaning Mom and Dad's house after they passed away, Kathy came across an old chest. As she began going through the contents, she discovered several items of memorabilia from Dad's ministry including one of his Bibles, sermon notes and an itinerary of a series of revivals. As I browsed through them, I reflected on many tremendous revivals Dad conducted during his tent evangelism ministry. I actually remembered hearing some of the messages of the notes in his notebook. Needless to say, I had a similar emotion as did David. My spirit was blessed and my faith was strengthened. I was able to press on through the difficult situation, and God was glorified. "Ah there is none like this!"

One of the messages I found in the sermon notes that day was entitled, "Your Last Tent Meeting." As mentioned earlier, much of Dad's ministry was that of a tent evangelist and we traveled all over the country conducting tent revivals. This message was one that reminded those in attendance, and hearing over the radio, that whether you come to this tent meeting or not, one day you will have a tent meeting. He was referring to the tent meeting that occurs at funerals where family, friends and the pastor gather to say good bye to you before the casket is lowered into the grave. His point was that in this tent meeting you will be the preacher, because it is your life that will speak to those in attendance. What will your life say and what impact will your past have on the future and most importantly, your eternal future.

Satan never gives up on accusing us of our past. He may be at your last tent meeting. In Jude Chapter 9, there is an account of a dispute between Satan and the archangel Michael at Moses' grave. Satan wanted Moses' body. Why? Some Bible scholars believe Satan wanted to resist Moses being raised to eternal life and chain him to his past due to his murdering of the Egyptian (Exodus 2:12) and his sin at Meribah (Deuteronomy 32;51). In this encounter, the archangel Michael would not allow it and said, "The Lord rebuke you."

Rest assured Satan will persistently try to chain us to our past. The archangel Michael gives us an amazing model as to how to deal with Satan in this matter. He did not take it on himself to intervene, but deferred to the name of the Lord. When Satan tries to chain us to our past, all we have to do is point to the cross and the name of the Lord, and remind him who our heavenly father is. He that the Son has set free is free indeed! Clink!

Keys to unlock the Chains of the Past

Pray to Lord for Him to snap the chains of the past.

Look to the future and let go of failures of the past.

Forgive yourself for mistakes of the past.

Behave in the way you believe the future will be.

Name your future in a positive light.

Let go of tradition, if tradition didn't work for you.

Learn from the negative outcomes of the past.

Fall back on positive outcomes of the past.

Chapter 6

Chain of Bad Attitudes

Let the words of my mouth, and the meditations of my heart,
be acceptable in thy sight, O Lord,
my strength and my redeemer.
Psalm 19:14 (KJV)

Bad attitudes are toxic to the environment we live in. When people have a bad attitude it affects their speech, countenance, demeanor, posture, physical, mental, emotional and spiritual capacity. When they walk in a room, it permeates the whole atmosphere. Conversely, the opposite is true when someone who is positive, enthusiastic and energetic walks in the room.

So where do bad attitudes come from? It has been said that it is easier to catch a bad attitude than it is to catch a cold. Not only can we catch a bad attitude, we can also be a carrier of a bad attitude that spreads to people around us. We can catch a bad attitude by surrounding ourselves with people that are always negative and complaining. If we are not diligent, we can allow that to penetrate our being to develop a bad attitude within us. Then we go spreading the bad attitude like a bad cold. Good people can catch a bad attitude and end up going sideways rather than forward toward the goals.

If we allow it, bad attitudes can come by responding to external sources inappropriately. Feeling unappreciated, being criticized, persecuted, being a victim of gossip, unhappy at work, family issues, and the list could go on, are common culprits. Life happens and it can be expected that we will encounter frustrating situations in our life. Frustration is normal, but can be looked at as a positive thing because it usually means we are trying to do something and meeting resistance. If we do not face frustration, we are probably settling for the status quo. Frustration can be the fuel to propel us to find a solution, or it can be a barrier that causes us to give up. The fact is, however, that we can choose how we are going to respond to these external forces.

Additionally, we can generate a bad attitude from within our own being by complaining aloud, and defaulting to negative thoughts in our mental capacity. Too often we fall into the habit of automatically declaring it is too hot, it is too cold, oh my it's raining, too much of this, not enough of that and so on. It is one thing to have a negative thought, but it is detrimental to speak it out loud. We need to filter our thoughts with no response or convert it to a positive reaction. Nothing is really gained by speaking negatively and complaining. Lou Holtz, a legendary football coach said, "It does no good to tell other people your problems because 90 percent of the people you tell don't care and the other 10 percent are happy you are having problems." The most harm done is to the person complaining, not the ones being complained to.

When I was the principal at Theodore Middle School, I had an employee who was a very hard worker, but he had the propensity to use a bad word every once in a while. I explained to him that it was inappropriate, especially working around children. I suggested that when he had the urge to use a bad word to substitute it with the word "bubbles." One day not long after that, he was working in my office and accidently hit his thumb with the hammer while hanging a blind. He dropped the hammer, and ran around the room shouting, "bubbles, bubbles, bubbles!!" We both laughed at the end and I congratulated him on his progress in that matter. We can train ourselves to default to an alternative expression to avoid the negative chain of events.

Who wants to be around a sour puss? How can we witness to the goodness of God when we are continuously complaining? People around us can begin to doubt God's blessings, if we are constantly dwelling on things that go wrong. It can be toxic to our relationships with our family, coworkers, and friends. How can we complain so much and then try to witness to those same people about the goodness of God. From our mental dimension (head brain) we choose to complain by verbalizing negative thoughts. Verbalizing negative thoughts develops a bad habit in our mental process to default to the negative on every situation. Not only is verbalizing negativity bad for those around us, but it is worse for us, because we hear it and internalize it. When we hear ourselves complain, it gets in our heart. Over time, we fill our heart brain with so much negativity it overflows out of our mouth and our emotional capacity (heart brain) speaks it and eventually becomes a cyclical process that creates our disposition. Luke 6:43-46 declares *for it is out of the abundance of the heart that the mouth speaks.*

Satan is also listening, not only do we hear negative words, but Satan hears them as well. He can't read our mind or thoughts, but he can hear what we say. He delights in hearing our negative state of mind and it gives him inroads to cause us more problems. He is an expert at attacking our weaknesses.

> *Blessed are ye, when men shall revile you and persecute you, and shall say all manner of evil against you falsely, for my sake. Rejoice, and be exceeding glad: for great is your reward in heaven: for so persecuted they the prophets which were before you.*
> Matthew 5:11-12 (KJV)

When we realize that we are not part of this world, things get a little more relaxed in our being. Frustration can occur when we are trying to be accepted or maneuver through this world's system. If we are living for Christ and abiding by Christ-like principals, we can expect to be hated without cause. Jesus said, "If they hated me, they will hate you."

Hate towards us is normal, so just put it all in perspective and not wrestle with it in our being anymore. Recognize that our enemy is Satan, not the people or situations he is using against us. It is easy for us to give God the glory for the good things he has done in our lives. For example, when someone is prayed for and they are healed, the people praying didn't heal them, God did it. So when someone is talking bad and trying to hurt you, it is not them. It is Satan. If we can grip this concept, we will be less likely to develop a bad attitude toward that person or situation.

Stay away from Mrs. Pafpoofnic, Mr. Derailit (*fictional names to exemplify negative individuals we encounter*) and the other misery evangelist we all face from time to time. They love to spread misery, gloom, despair and agony. We should get away from it and run to what gives us joy and allow it to rejuvenate us. To run to what gives us joy, we should pause during those frustrated moments and breathe in deeply as we think on things that are lovely to us right now and enjoy the moment. Then breathe out with a big *ahhh*. It has been said, "It is not what happens to you, but through you that defines you."

> *Let no corrupt communication proceed out of your mouth, but that which is good to the use of edifying, that it may minister grace unto the hearers.*
>
> Ephesians 4:29 (KJV)

We impact the way things go around us based on our own attitude. In the field of education, I have observed the key to success is the teacher's enthusiasm. I have seen students who come into a teacher's room not really wanting to be there, but due to the teacher's enthusiasm and positive attitude, they became invigorated and motivated. One degree between 211 and 212 degrees Fahrenheit changes everything in the physical environment. That one degree changes the state of water from simmering to boiling thus creating steam. In the classroom, it wasn't because the content of the lesson suddenly became better, but the teachers added that one more degree with his/her positive attitude to transform the state of the lesson from simmering to steam. The classroom example is only a model of what is possible in our daily interactions. Our contribution to the interaction in our environment can be that one degree to tick up or down.

God wants us to be the one degree that glorifies Him rather than the simmering pot that holds us back due to our complaining. If we buy into God's plan, we will want to please him and not complain. The Children of Israel turned a short trip into a 40 year journey due to their complaining. God became angry at them regarding their complaining. Even though they had seen his mighty works of deliverance, they complained over and over again. Ultimately, God declared that everyone 20 years or older would not possess the land. We do not want God to ultimately give up on us. Has He not blessed us? Has He not been faithful? Does He not want to lead us into our promised land? Of course, He does. Focus on God's blessings, and resist putting on the chain that will prohibit us from possessing the promise land He has for us.

It has been said that Eagles soar, but ducks quack. I have observed that people's conversations fall in to one of those categories. We are either soaring or quacking. Which conversation do you want to be around, and better yet, which category does our conversation fall into? All of this quaking can become annoying as people complain about every little thing. I want to say enough, already!

There are references in the Bible to eagles. My favorite is in Isaiah 40:31, that indicates those who wait on the Lord shall mount up with wings as eagles. We can fly above the noise and accomplish our purpose without complaining and that speaks tremendously to our confidence in God. Recently, I was standing on the deck of our house on the river and noticed a beautiful bald eagle in the top of a tree. After a few minutes, he took flight effortlessly over the top of the trees. It was breath taking. That is what I want to be.

> *But they that wait upon the Lord shall renew*
> *their strength; they shall mount up with wings*
> *as eagles; they shall run, and not be weary; and*
> *they shall walk, and not faint.*
>
> Isaiah 40:31 (KJV)

All of us can fall into the habit of quacking instead of soaring and should be conscious of what we speak and how it affects our attitude, as well as others around us. As a constant reminder to me and others that we are either quacking or soaring, I have a toy stuffed duck that quacks when you squeeze it, and beside it a very pretty porcelain bald eagle. Occasionally, I have to squeeze the duck while someone is talking. Sometimes they have to squeeze it for me, if we begin to quack toxic conversation into the environment. I use this as my *quack-a-lytic converter*. This works on the same principal as the catalytic converter that is required in vehicles beginning in 1975. A catalytic converter is an exhaust emission control device that converts toxic gases and pollutants in exhaust gas internal combustion engines into less toxic pollutants. This device was first used in the United States to comply with the U.S. Environmental Protection Agency regulations to reduce toxic emissions. Interestingly, there is a three way process to combine oxygen with carbon monoxide (CO) and unburned hydrocarbons (HC) to produce carbon dioxide (CO_2) and water (H_2O) and reduce oxides of nitrogen (NOx).

> *Do all things without murmurings and quest-*
> *ionings.*
>
> Philippians 2:14 (ASV}

We, too, should deliberately and consciously engage in a three step process (quack-a-lytic converter) in our conversations to reduce our toxic emissions into the environment. Before we spew out negative thoughts, comments and criticism, we should process it through our Head Brain (Mental Capacity), Heart Brain (emotional and spiritual) and our Gut Brain (physical) to make sure it fits our real values, passions, and appropriate actions. Taking time to filter our thoughts will likely reduce toxic emissions.

> *Give thanks in all circumstances; for this is the*
> *will of God in Christ Jesus for you.*
>
> 1 Thessalonians 5:18 (ESV)

A few years back, Kathy and I went on a cruise. On the first morning, we went down to eat breakfast. Even though there were several entrances to the breakfast area, we noticed there was a long line at one of the particular entrances. Out of curiosity, we got in the longer line. When we got to the front of the line there was a cruise line employee at the door spraying each person's hands as they walked by. As he sprayed our hands, with a big smile on his face, he said to each person, "Happy Happy, Washy Washy!!" Needless to say, it made us feel good and at each meal from then on, we (along with hundreds of other passengers) sought out the Happy Happy, Washy Washy line. On the last night of the cruise, there was a big gala at which they introduced the ship's staff. One by one as each person was introduced there was a polite round of applause. After everyone had been introduced, from the back of the stage a little guy skipped up to the line where the staff who had just been introduced was standing. Yes, he was shouting, "Happy Happy, Washy Washy." A thunderous round of applause erupted with a standing ovation for this employee for several minutes. Mr. Happy Happy, Washy Washy is a prime example of how one person can change the atmosphere of an entire ship.

So how can we have the mind of Christ and still complain and demonstrate a bad attitude? James 3:11 declares that bitter and sweet cannot come out of the same spring. Additionally, Matthew 12:24 tells us that *out of the abundance of the heart, the mouth speaks.* By filling our heart with good things, and drawing close to God by reading His word, prayer, and giving praise, our spring will be one that permeates the atmosphere around us with sweet water that is observed through our words and deeds. When we do this, we will hear the sound "Clink" as the chain of a bad attitude falls to the ground.

Keys to unlock the Chain of a Bad Attitude

🔑 Pray for the Lord to snap the chain of a bad attitude.

🔑 Fill your heart with good things.

🔑 Build physical, mental, emotional, and spiritual capacity.

🔑 Build a space between the stimulus and response, in that space...

🔑 Filter the words you say, or listen to through your head, heart and gut.

🔑 Take responsibility for mistakes without blaming others.

🔑 Forgive yourself for the mistakes you have made, make corrections and press on.

🔑 Be Generous. Fill other people's bucket with time and resources.

🔑 Soar above negative conversations and sarcasm.

🔑 Run toward things that give you joy and away from negative, toxic environments.

🔑 Let go of bad habits. Do not allow your thoughts to default to the negative position.

🔑 Do not worry about others' opinions of you. Their opinion doesn't define you.

🔑 Find the positive in every situation. There is one!

🔑 Live in the moment and enjoy the ride.

🔑 Give thanks to God in every circumstance.

Chapter 7

Chain of Gossip

Evil people relish malicious conversation;
the ears of liars itch for dirty gossip.
Proverbs 17:4 (MSG)

Just as lying is one of the seven things hated by God, gossiping is listed as one of the seven things God hates listed in Proverbs 6:16-19. In this passage, God indicates he hates the sowing of discord among the brethren. I heard my dad say, "A lie can make its way around the world before the truth can even get its pants on." With social media, that statement is more accurate than ever. Gossip is different from lying because the information being spread could possibly be true. Even if a statement is true, if it sows discord and hurt when repeated, then it is gossip. The scripture tells us in Proverbs 18:21 that there are consequences for being a participant in gossip.

Death and life are in the power of the tongue:
and they that love it shall eat the fruit thereof.

Proverbs 18:21 (KJV)

It is generally agreed upon that gossiping is a negative thing and we understand we should not gossip. However, we should note that not only should we not gossip, but we should not listen to gossip either. The part of the verse that says, "and" those who love it (listen to it) shall eat the fruit there of.

Gossip is equal to murder. It may not physically harm anyone, but it murders their reputation. Sometimes it is referred to as character assassination.

You shall not spread a false report. You shall
not join hands with a wicked man to be a mali-
cious witness.

Exodus 23:1 (ESV)

It is easy to get pulled into a gossip session. One technique I have found useful to end the session without getting involved, is to ask the person speaking the gossip, "Have you spoken with this person about your concerns?" If they say no, I suggest that we bring that person in to the conversation and ask them directly. It is amazing to see the conversation change as quickly as it does. No matter how hard we may try, gossip has a way of prevailing.

Sometimes we are victims of hurtful gossip and slander. Our natural instinct is to respond and get in the middle of the controversy. In these cases, responding perpetuates the mess. As Christians, we do not have to defend ourselves with arguments and controversy. God will fight for us. The scripture tells us in Ephesians 6:13 that when having done all, stand. From a Biblical perspective, we see that attacks against us actually propel us to higher levels of success. The best example of this fact is when Jesus was crucified in an attempt to get rid of His teaching. We know what happened after that.

I love playing in the pool with my grandchildren and sometimes we will end up throwing a beach ball around. I have noticed that it is difficult to submerge a beach ball under water. It seems the harder you push it down, the harder it pushes back. I have occasionally been successful pushing it under, but as soon as it is released, it shoots up out of the water higher than it would have if we had just left it alone. It is a natural phenomenon of physics that the farther under water it is pushed down, the higher it shoots out of the water. When people try to push us down, there is a supernatural phenomenon of the Holy Spirit that we will soar higher than before.

> *A new command I give you: Love one another, as*
> *I have loved you, so you must love one another.*
> *By this everyone will know that you are my dis-*
> *ciples, if you love one another.*
>
> John 13:34-35 (NIV)

How can we claim to be loving-hearted Christians if we gossip? John 13:35 declares, *it is by the love we show that people*

CLINK

know we are his disciples. It is out of the abundance of the heart that our mouth speaks. What is coming out of our mouth is a product of what is in our heart. When we spread gossip or listen to gossip, not only are we bringing hurt to the person we are gossiping about, but we are hurting our own testimony by not showing the love that Jesus has shown us. The scripture is clear that there is death and life in the power of the tongue. If we choose to use our tongue for negative words, it can lead to death. Gossip can lead to slander, broken relationships, and loss of life.

One prevalent issue in our society is the problem of suicide (more on this later). Close to 800,000 people die globally due to suicide every year and it is the 10th leading cause of death in the United States. The most common underlying factor for victims of suicide is major depression. Our words can be a tipping point for those we are in contact with. If we are gossiping and belittling people, we are contributing to their depression. How tragic it would be to have a part in causing serious grief to someone by spreading hurtful things, true or not. However, if we speak positively, it is possible that our positive words can be the key that unlocks the chain of someone else's prison. Christ has come so that we can have life and more abundant life. Our words should reflect the life that Christ brings rather than death that a slanderous tongue brings.

I remember playing those games where one person is given a statement to repeat to the person beside them and that person should repeat it to the person beside them, and so on until the process has worked itself all the way around the room. Then the last person would share what the statement was and then we compare it with the original statement. Wow. There was generally no comparison and the group would laugh and wonder how in the world it could have gotten off so badly.

Unfortunately, this happens in real life with real people and more serious situations, especially with the prevalence of social media. One sure way to avoid becoming entangled in the chain of gossip is to avoid it altogether. Just do not listen to it, read it, or share it. The person listening to the gossip is just as guilty as the one who spreads it. Sooner or later, as the saying goes, it all comes home to roost. When we speak against someone, it releases the possibility of bad things for our own life. Proverbs 26:2 declares a curse does not come without a cause. A bird will fly thousands of miles and end up in the same nest at the same location in the same tree. Something inside it draws it to that location. Proverbs 26:2 is saying that a curse doesn't mysteriously fall on us, rather it is drawn to us and lands in our spiritual nest.

> *Like a fluttering sparrow or a darting swallow,*
> *an undeserved curse does not come to rest.*
> Proverbs 26:2 (NIV)

To avoid slipping into a pitfall of gossiping, we should develop a habit of reversing negative conversation into a positive topic. If someone begins speaking negatively about someone else, begin immediately to think of a positive response about that person. We will be held accountable for the words we speak and should be certain that they are positive and uplifting words. We should listen with a spiritual ear to detect the sound of gossip coming to us, or through us, and end it immediately. The choice is ours. We can hear the noise of gossip, or the sound "Clink" as the chain of gossip falls off of us.

Keys to unlock the Chain of Gossip

- Pray that the Lord will snap the chain of gossip.

- Avoid speaking idle words.

- Do not listen to idle words.

- Do not speak negative things about others, even if it is true.

- Do not listen to negative things about others, even if is true.

- Remove yourself from the presence of conversation that leads to gossip.

- Show love and respect to others in your conversations.

- Convert gossiping conversations to more positive conversations.

- Fill our hearts with positive things: mentally, physically, spiritually and emotionally.

Chapter 8

Chain of Jealousy

You shall not covet your neighbor's house;
you shall not covet your neighbor's wife, or his male servant,
or his female servant, or his ox, or his donkey,
or anything that is your neighbors.
Exodus 20:17 (ESV)

Jealousy is an inherent part of human nature. It is natural to experience jealousy from time to time, but there is a difference between an emotional feeling of jealousy and morbid jealousy. Morbid jealousy is the chain that binds us. However, an emotional feeling of jealousy can grow into an unhealthy morbid jealousy if not overcome. Morbid jealousy leads us to act in a harmful, damaging way to ourselves and others. Song of Solomon 8:6 tells us that *jealousy is cruel as the grave and coals of fire that have a vehement flame.*

The chain of jealousy has a presence throughout the Bible and is still prevalent in our world today. People are hindered from progressing in many areas of their lives because they are worried about who will get the credit, or who has what and how much, etc. In the workplace, church, family, and society in general, the chain of jealousy destroys harmonious relationships and progress.

From the beginning of biblical days, jealousy was present resulting in a rough start and it originated from Satan's desire to be God instead of a servant of God. Satan was the highest of all the angels, but he wasn't happy. He desired to be God and rule the universe. God cast Satan out of heaven as a fallen angel (Revelation 12:1-12). The Bible doesn't give us a specific time this occurred, but logic will tell us it happened sometime between the creation of angels, and his first appearance with Adam and Eve in the Garden of Eden. Adam and Eve fell to the temptation, through jealousy, brought by Satan, which led to mankind's separation from God. It all started with jealousy and it continued throughout the Bible and still does to this day.

Another notable example of jealousy in the Bible is found in the treatment of Joseph by his brothers in 2 Kings Chapter 13. Jacob, Joseph's father, held Joseph to be special and knew he would be a great leader. Jacob gave Joseph the coat of many colors that became a symbol of the favoritism between this father and son. Perhaps it also symbolized the prophecy given in Joseph's dream that he would someday be in a position of royalty, ruling over his family and others. This gift, however, further aggravated the jealousy already felt by Joseph's ten older brothers and was the first step of destined events that resulted in Joseph being sold into slavery. Joseph's difficulties along the way, caused by his brothers' jealousy, propelled him into a position of second in command of all of Egypt and that allowed him to be instrumental in saving an entire nation. Additionally, it fulfilled the covenant between God and Abraham, Joseph's great-grandfather, providing that Abraham's seed would bring about many nations with kings and rulers among them (Genesis 17:4).

Another example of Jealousy is found in the account of Saul's actions toward David. David became highly favored with the people as he performed mightily in battle. When Saul heard them singing a song with the lyrics "Saul has killed his thousands, but David has killed ten thousand" he became jealous and set out to kill David. In the end, however, David became king and Saul completely lost out with God.

All of us have a story and song. Satan is jealous of that song and he will set out to destroy us as well. Often he will use family, friends and other unexpected sources, who become jealous and work against us. Sometimes when people become jealous, they set out to hurt people they should be learning from.

Set me as a seal upon thine heart, as a seal upon thine arm: for love is strong as death; jealousy is cruel as the grave: the coals thereof are coals of fire, which hath a most vehement flame.
Song of Solomon 8:6 (KJV)

In the cases of Saul's jealousy toward David, and Joseph's brother's jealousy toward him, their jealousy brought hardship on themselves. We have to guard against becoming jealous toward others. It typically comes back on us in a negative way. When we fret over what we do not have, compared to what others have, or become envious of others' success, we are vulnerable to the possibility of jealousy walking through the door resulting in negative consequence in our own life.

The chain of jealousy works both ways. Sometimes we are the victim of jealousy, other times we are overcome with jealousy toward others. Jealousy shows up in the workplace, among family members, church members, church staff, and anywhere there are people. It is an effective tool of Satan to disrupt God's plan for our lives. When we are victims of jealous acts, be of good cheer; God is with us and He will turn bad actions into blessings. It is a mistake to take matters in our own hands. Romans Chapter 2 declares that if we condemn such people, we are as bad as they and we are condemning ourselves. By taking matters into our own hands, we are placing the chain of jealousy on ourselves. By faith we have to release the outcomes based on the actions of others into God's hands. When we release it to Him, we have released ourselves. Clink!

Keys to unlock the Chain of Jealousy

Pray for the Lord to snap the chain of jealousy.

Be content with what we have. We have to recognize that God loves us and desires to give us his best. If we remain faithful and follow the plan, in due time it will come.

🗝 Recognize we cannot change other people or what God is doing through them. We can only accept where we are and ask God to help us to work with them from where they are.

🗝 When we are victims of jealous attacks, remember that God will turn things intended for bad to our good, and fulfill his perfect plan.

🗝 Guard against being jealous of others. That emotional feeling leads to negative effects mentally, physically, emotionally and spiritually. Left unchecked, it could result in our reacting to a situation that will only make things worse.

🗝 Be prepared. Jealousy is coming your way. Be proactive! Shore up spiritually by reading the word, fasting and praying.

🗝 Don't worry about who gets the credit, just focus on reaching the goal.

Chapter 9

Chain of Impatience

Be still before the LORD and wait patiently for him;
fret not yourself over the one who prospers in his way,
over the man who carries out evil devices!
Psalms 37:7 (ESV)

I once heard of a person who prayed, "Lord give me patience and I need it NOW!" As funny as it sounds, we all need to be patient and that means now. Being impatient has caused many problems in people's lives. Often we respond too quickly to situations and it leads to difficulty. I can honestly say that most of the time when I jump to a conclusion or react too quickly to a situation, the result is usually not good. It has been said that the early bird gets the worm, but the second mouse gets the cheese. When we jump in too quickly, we can end up like the first mouse stuck in the trap, rather than nibbling on the cheese like the second mouse.

In 2018, The University of Alabama won the SEC Football Championship with a victory over Georgia. This win secured them the number one seed in the National Championship Playoffs. By virtue of being the number one seed, they could choose between going to the Cotton Bowl in Dallas, or the Orange Bowl in Miami. I just knew they would choose to go to Dallas since it would be the closer venue for them and the fans. With that in mind, I hastily went online and purchased my tickets for the game before the actual announcement had been made. My intention was to purchase the tickets early before the cost increased too much. Ooops! When the announcement was made, Alabama had made the choice to go to the Orange Bowl rather than the Cotton Bowl, and there I was with tickets to the wrong game. Kathy was not at all happy with me. I put the tickets up for sale and every day or so Kathy would ask me if I had sold the tickets yet and I got that look (*guys you know what I'm talking about*)! Finally, just hours before the game, I sold the tickets and it all worked out. I learned a valuable lesson about being impatient and the consequences that can result from hasty actions.

In the Bible there are many examples of individuals becoming impatient and taking matters into their own hands. In each case, their impatience led to negative consequences. Here are a few examples.

1. Esau got impatient and sold his birthright. Now in the Bible we see the lineage being Abraham, Isaac,

and Jacob, but it could have been Abraham, Isaac and Esau (Genesis 25).

2. Abraham and Sarah got impatient about having a child that God promised. This led to the birth of Ishmael, then Isaac. The impatience demonstrated in this case resulted in a conflict that exists to this day.

3. Saul got impatient, because Samuel was supposed to meet him in seven days, but was late. In fear of being attacked by Philistines, Saul made a sacrifice asking for God's help. Samuel said, "You have done a foolish thing. If you had done what God commanded you, the Lord would let your family rule over Israel forever, but since you disobeyed, your kingdom will not continue." (1 Samuel 13)

4. When Moses went to the mountain, and was gone for so long, Aaron and the people got impatient and made an idol in the shape of a golden calf made from their earrings. Had Moses not intervened, they would have faced the wrath of an angry God (Exodus 32).

5. God instructed the Israelites not to go forth and fight the Amorites. In their rebellion, they went forth and engaged in battle and the Amorites came out of the hills like a swarm of bees and beat them down. When they came back defeated and weeping, God ignored them and turned a deaf ear to their cry (Deuteronomy 1).

I love the popular scripture in Jeremiah 29:11 where God declares His plans to bless and prosper the people. But wait a minute! In the previous verse, Jeremiah 29:10, he said AFTER 70 years he would visit them and fulfill his promise. From this passage we see that even though God has a plan for our lives, he also has a time line. We have to be patient and move according to his plan.

In the Old Testament, the Israelites relied on God for their provision and direction. They followed the cloud and when it moved, they would move. When the cloud stopped and hovered over the tabernacle, they would set up camp and remain as long it hovered there. Sometimes it hovered a few days and other times it would be several weeks. Wouldn't it be great in our lives today if our moves were directed in such obvious ways? But many times it is not clear whether we should move, stay, wait or go.

While there is no cloud to guide us these days, God does still give us direction through his word, prayer, circumstances and even miraculous things around us. In order for us to hear him, or see the cloud, we must take intentional action to seek his will through our daily devotion with prayer and Bible study. We will not hear his voice, or see the cloud so to speak, if we are too far away from the source. As we seek his will, we have to keep pressing on as God leads, and be patient when he says "wait." God desires to bless us, but many times due to disobedience and hindrances from Satan, our blessing can be delayed. If we give up and move on to something or some other place, we will miss our blessing when it arrives to the place we left.

A good example of our answer being delayed is found in Daniel Chapters 9 and 10.

In these chapters, Daniel was pleading with the Lord for favor over events he had seen in a vision. For 21 days he fasted and prayed. Then Gabriel came and gave him insight. Gabriel indicated to Daniel that he heard his prayer when he first prayed, but was delayed due to spiritual warfare in the heavenlies.

Sometimes our blessing or answer is delayed due to other people's failure to be obedient as a result of spiritual warfare. But just as Daniel discovered, we have to keep fasting, praying and waiting for God to move on our behalf. He wants us to trust him during the times of waiting. Even though he is going before us to pave the way, the road will not always be smooth and free from a few pot holes. If we move ahead of God, we are on our own and reposition ourselves away from his covering, protection and perfect will. God will allow us to do this, but we are on our own. Conversely, when we fail to move when he moves, we can miss opportunities he desires for us to enjoy. We have to realize that for everything there is a season. When it is not our season for one thing, it is a season for another. God's timing is vital to our success.

> *For everything there is a season, and a time to every purpose under heaven.*
> Ecclesiastes 3:1 (KJV)

Satan is happy for us to get out of step with God's timing. Rest assured he is planning and plotting against us and he will look to pick the perfect time for his attack. A good example of this is found in Mark 14. In this passage, the chief priest and scribes were planning how they might take Jesus and put him to death, but they agreed not to do it during the feast of the Passover because there were too many people and it would cause an uproar. They waited and selected a more sneaky time while he was in Gethsemane and his disciples were asleep. Jesus asked them why they chose that time because he had been with them daily in the temple. We can rest assured that the enemy is plotting against us as well, and he will pick the most opportune time to attack us. Satan is plotting his timing against you, and God is planning his time for you. If we follow God's plan, in due time, He will foil Satan's plot.

> *But they that wait upon the Lord shall renew*
> *their strength; they shall mount up with wings*
> *as eagles; they shall run, and not be weary; and*
> *they shall walk, and not faint.*
>
> Isaiah 40:31 (KJV)

In December 1994, our car was broken into in the church parking lot while we were rehearsing the choir at Mobile First Assembly of God. Damage to the car and items stolen, including some Christmas presents for the family, resulted in approximately $1,000.00 in loss. It was particularly disappointing to us because this happened while we were doing something related to our ministry at the church. We reported it to the police and followed the legal steps needed. We chalked it up as an attack by Satan on our finances and a hurtful distraction during final preparations for the upcoming Christmas program. We never really thought about it again, but let it go into God's hands.

On April 19, 2017, 23 years later, out of the clear blue sky, we received a call from Victim Services informing us that the individual had been caught earlier and restitution was being made. A few days later we received a check and the information regarding future payments. Through this incident, Kathy and I learned that in due time God will make the crooked path straight (Isaiah 45:2). We can rest assured that when we are being faithful to our calling, God will have our back. Of course, Satan will try to get us to believe that God has forgotten about us or doesn't care about our situation. It may take longer than we would like, but in due time God will come through for us. With that knowledge, we can press on and release the tough situations into God's hand and block the fiery darts of Satan with the shield of Faith. Additionally, when we realize that God's miracles of rescue and deliverance are not things of the past, but are at work in our lives, we can be patient and allow God's power to be manifested today.

For the past several years I have taken my daily physical, mental, emotional and spiritual preparation very seriously with a strict regime. I have thanked God for the motivation to press on, but at times I have asked Him, "What am I preparing for? Is there some big thing ahead that I need to be prepared for?" Recently, he spoke this to my heart and said, "I am preparing you for today. If you are prepared and effective for what you have to do today, I can guide you properly to what I have for you tomorrow." If we approach our preparation with that assurance in mind, we can get ready for today and leave our tomorrows up to Him.

In David's lifetime he spent a great deal of time waiting. He waited 15 years from the time he was anointed by Samuel to become king, before he actually became king over Judah. There was another seven years before he became king over all of Israel. This totaled over 20 years for God's plan in David's life to come to fruition. In the case of Joshua in the battle with the Amorites, He made the sun stand still for 24 hours to provide enough daylight for Joshua's army to win the battle.

God slows things down many times for our own protection and well-being. I missed a fatal accident by 30 seconds recently and I realized it could have been me. God uses every second to guide our lives. In this case, 30 seconds changed everything. So why be impatient? God can do marvelous things in a whole day, week, or a year in working on our behalf. Even if it gets down to the last 30 seconds, he will be an on time God. Even when it appears that time has run out, God will do whatever it takes to accomplish his will. Be calm and avoid being impatient because God is in control.

In the case of Noah, the process to build the ark took 120 years. I can only imagine the self-discipline required day by day to accomplish the task for each day in order to reach the ultimate goal. During that time period, it would be tempting to question God about building an ark in preparation for a flood when the sun was shining, not to mention the criticism he received from peers. I can only imagine if I were in that position, Kathy wanting to know when I was going to finish that project going on in the front yard.

Noah did finish building the ark and all of his family and animals entered in. God closed the door behind him in perfect timing and the rain fell for 40 days and 40 nights. After 150 days the ark came to rest on the mountains of Ararat. After another 4 months, Noah opened a window and released a raven and later doves to see if the water had receded. It had not, so he waited. Finally, after 2 more months the earth was dry and God opened the door with instructions to leave the boat. If Noah had been impatient and left the boat earlier through the window, he would have perished. From this we know that God opens doors and closes doors in his due time. We should walk through doors he opens and not attempt to go through doors he closes. I have learned when he closes a door, not to go through the window because there may be nothing on the other side to catch us. Instead of hearing the sound *clink*, as He unlocks the door, we will hear the sound of *splashing* when we fall in waters over our head.

Keys to unlock the Chain of Impatience

Pray for the Lord to snap the chain of impatience.

Keep your eyes on the goals God has birthed in you.

Realize God's timing is perfect and rarely fits into our way of thinking.

Trust in God even though you can't see the future.

Take care of what has to be done today. Day by day you will move closer to the goal.

Relax in the knowledge that in due time God will make the crooked path straight.

Follow the plan and He will foil plot.

Know that your blessing is on the way and stay in position to receive it.

Chapter 10

Chain of Greed

But those who desire to be rich fall into temptation,
into a snare, into many senseless and harmful desires
that plunge people into ruin and destruction.
1 Timothy 6:9 (ESV)

In our society today there is a mindset of obtaining and hoarding more and more possessions. We buy things and then get some more in a few months when a new fad comes out. After a while, we run out of room and rent a storage space, or have a yard sale to make room for some more stuff. When it is all said and done, we find pursing pleasure and contentment in things such as possessions, reputation, and personal indulgence leaves a feeling of pain and emptiness.

Wanting things for ourselves is innate in all of us to some degree. Mom says that when I was a baby there was a period of time when they would give my older brother a gift and I would be content to be able to play with the box that it came in. This box was fine for a while, but when I got a little older, they gave me the box and I threw the box down. I exclaimed, "NO BOX! NO BOX!" That episode evidenced my first awareness of being selfish, because I wanted something for ME!

We have to face the issue of greed versus need. We obviously have essential needs in our lives for sustaining ourselves. We have a responsibility to take care of ourselves and families through the means with what God has blessed us. Philippians 4:19 tells us that God will supply for all our needs according to his riches in glory. He knows what we need and often what he knows we need is different from what we think we need. Sometimes we want to hoard and gather things that we think we need, but God knows it may not be good for us.

In the materialistic, entitlement age we live in, it is easy to get caught up in believing we have to have the best and newest i-phone, car, house, or just "keep up with the Jones'." This frame of mind can lead us down the road of developing a greedy attitude. It has been said, "The person who is not happy with a little, will not be happy with more." They will always want a little bit more. Happiness is not based on material things. Instead, it is based on God's blessings. God, accompanied with what he has blessed us with, is enough. Apostle Paul admonishes us in Philippians 4:11 to be content with whatever we have.

> *I am not saying this because I am in need, for I have learned to be content in whatever the circumstances.*
>
> Philippians 4:11 (NIV)

And he said to them, "Take care, and be on your
guard against all covetousness, for one's life does
not consist in the abundance of his possessions."
Luke 12:15 (ESV)

Examples of greed are common throughout the Bible. One biblical example of greed disrupting an individual life is found in 2 Kings Chapter 5. In this account we see that Naaman the leper went to Elisha to be healed from his leprosy (more on this later). After following the directions and being obedient to the directions Elisha gave him, Naaman was healed. Naaman was so grateful that he offered valuable gifts, but Elisha declined to accept them and sent Naaman on his way. However, Elisha's servant, having heard the offer of gifts and Elisha's not accepting them, devised a plan of greed. Elisha' servant intercepted Naaman on his journey home and lied to Naaman saying that Elisha had changed his mind and wanted to accept the gifts. Naaman gladly gave the gifts to the servant. In the end, Elisha's servant was exposed and he became stricken with leprosy, the very disease that Naaman had been delivered from.

Do nothing out of selfish ambition or vain conceit.
Rather, in humility value others above yourselves.
Philippians 2:3 (NIV)

Another biblical account of the act of greed is found in Acts Chapter 16. In this scripture, there was a girl possessed with a pythonic spirit that made a great deal of money for her masters by predicting the future. However, she began to heckle Paul and when he had enough, he cast out the spirit. When the girl's masters realized her ability to make them money was gone, they brought charges against Paul and Silas for causing a disturbance in the city. Their real motive was retaliation for disrupting their money making arrangement.

> *Now listen, you rich people, weep and wail because of the misery that is coming on you. Your wealth has rotted, and moths have eaten your clothes. Your gold and silver are corroded. Their corrosion will testify against you and eat your flesh like fire. You have hoarded wealth in the last days. Look! The wages you failed to pay the workers who mowed your fields are crying out against you. The cries of the harvesters have reached the ears of the Lord Almighty.*
>
> James 5:1-4 (NIV)

In another example in Acts Chapter 8, Simon offered the apostles money to buy power they possessed in order to make money. Peter replied, "May your money be destroyed with you for thinking God's gift can be bought." Unfortunately, this spirit exists today as we still see religious people trying to use God's power as a profit making event.

Another example of greed that chains us is that of failing to pay what we owe. We are obligated to pay our bills, pledges we have made, our tithes, and if we are an employer, pay our workers for the work done. Failure to do so will result in our being bound by the chain of sin. Deuteronomy 24:15 says that by doing so makes you guilty of sin.

> *You shall not oppress a hired servant who is poor and needy, whether he is of your brothers or one of the sojourners who are in your land within your towns. You shall give him his wages on the same day, before the sun sets (for he is poor and he counts on it), lest he cry against you to the Lord, and you be guilty of sin.*
> Deuteronomy 24:14-15 (ESV)

Additionally, Greed can manifest itself in family resolutions of an inheritance. Many times families are torn apart because of one or more family members deceiving or manipulating family inheritance for their own good.

> *An inheritance hastily gained (by greedy, unjust means) at the beginning Will not be blessed in the end.*
> Proverbs 20:21 (AMP)

We must not strive for prosperity and gain through fraud and greed. Instead, we should allow God to move in His season and the rain will fall on us in due time. Being greedy is a demonstration of a lack of faith. Everything we were supposed to receive in the past and what we should receive in the future is coming to us.

There is no need for us to be greedy. God has it worked out. And if we choose to be greedy through fraud, it is going to be transferred out of our account into the account of good people's account. If we truly believe God's word and walk in faith, we know that God is working on our behalf and he will supply our needs.

> *But seek first the kingdom of God and his righteousness, and all these things will be added to you.*
> Matthew 6:33 (ESV)

When Jesus told Peter to cast the net on the other side of the boat (John 21:6), Peter had to abandon his way of thinking and trust Jesus. Peter was the fishermen, and Jesus was the carpenter. Jesus was telling Peter, "I am going to bless you my way. Your way as a fisherman is not working." Sometimes our blessing doesn't come through normal channels and expectations. We should not question how God blesses us, just receive it when it comes and not fret if doesn't come the way we thought it would. It is up to God. Trust Him.

Our perceptions are not the same as God's. What looks like a blessing in our eyes, may not be to God, and vice versa. he can turn the green tree brown, and the brown tree green. God's blessings are just that, his blessings. We should never believe we are receiving financial blessings because of our own righteousness. No, it is because of God's promises and grace.

> *"All the trees of the forest will know that I the LORD bring down the tall tree and make the low*

*tree grow tall. I dry up the green tree and make
the dry tree flourish. I the LORD have spoken,
and I will do it."*

Ezekiel 17:24 (NIV)

We can find true prosperity by helping others and developing a sound financial plan in accordance to God's word. Greed may temporarily bring us money, but true prosperity comes from generosity. In Acts Chapter 3 we see where Peter and John went to the temple to pray and encountered a lame man who was begging for money. When the man asked them for money, Peter said, "I don't have any silver or gold, but I will give you what I have." He said, "In the name of Jesus Christ the Nazarene, get up and walk!" Then the lame man jumped up and began to walk. Likewise, God desires to use us to bless others. God blesses us so we can bless others. One sure way to sustain God's blessings is for us to allow his blessings to flow through us to other people.

So, what meaningful things can we give people in need? We can give of ourselves by giving our time, love, care and support. Matthew 16:25 declares that *whosoever would save his life will loses it, and whoever loses his life for my sake will find it.* In other words, only by giving ourselves up for others can we redeem ourselves. Only by giving ourselves away can we find ourselves.

Sometime, we have to step out in faith to be a blessing to others, even though we are already in need of a blessing ourselves. One example is the widow in the town of Zarephath (1 Kings 17). In this case, she used the last supply of ingredients she had to prepare a meal for Elijah. As a result, forever more, she had all she needed with plenty left over to sell. Everyone can give something. In Mark 12:44, there is another example where a lady gave her last penny. Even though it was only a penny, Jesus said she gave more than all the rest.

Additionally, we never know how our generous acts of helping others will come back to help us in the future. Sometimes we are paying it forward and do not even realize it. A great example of this principle is found in the account of Mephibosheth, (2 Samuel 4:4) who was Jonathan's son and Saul's grandson. In a time when Saul was trying to kill David, Jonathan intervened and helped David escape. Many years later when David was king, He sought out anyone related to Jonathan in order to bless them because he remembered him and what he had done for him. He brought Mephibosheth into the palace to eat at his table and provided for all of his needs for the rest of his life. In our lives we never know when an act of compassion or kindness will come back to help us in a time of need. The seeds we plant may not produce while we are alive, but in due time they will flourish.

Oh the joy that comes with giving and the blessings that follow; versus the negative feelings and the blocking of our blessing that accompanies acts of greed. We should develop our heart toward a feeling of compassion and translate that feeling into action in order to overcome greed. The heart brain feels compassion, the head brain recognizes what the situation needs, and the gut brain spurs us to action. It does no good to see a brother in need and tell him to have a nice day, keep warm, and not help in anyway.

Our failure to help others has negative consequences for us. A good example is the Dead Sea. The Dead Sea has many tributaries that flow into it, but none out. As a result, the water is a stagnant mess. If we are only recipients of blessings, and never let them out to others, our lives can become stagnant as well. Additionally, we will block our own blessing because God will block his ear to our prayers.

Whoso stoppeth his ears at the cry of the poor,
he also shall cry himself, but shall not be heard.
Proverbs 21:13 (KJV)

The flip side of greed can occur when we have been a victim of other's greedy actions. We do not have to worry because God is faithful to us. The Lord God gives the former rain and the latter rain in its season. Joel 2:23 says that he will come to us like latter rain and the former rain and he will restore to us all that we should have had in the past, as well as what we are due in the future. We do not have to take matters into our hands. When we take matters into our own hands, we are putting another version of the chain of greed on ourselves. Let God handle it because he has a plan. Proverbs 13:22 speaks of a transfer of wealth from the evil ones to God's people. Although there is debate as to how or when this will happen, as God's people, we do not have worry or be greedy because it is all going to work out. The chain of greed will be broken in its season. I would much rather hear the sound "Clink" as the chain of greed falls off, as opposed to the "Jingle' sound of money in my pocket gained through deceit and selfish acts.

Keys to unlock the Chain of Greed

Pray for the Lord to snap the chain of greed.

Seek first the kingdom of God and the rest will be added unto you.

Pay tithes and give to the ministry.

Avoid the Dead Sea Effect. What you keep is your harvest, what you give is your seed.

Be honest without deceit.

Do not try to keep up with the Jones'.

Pay your bills.

Pay your employees.

Show compassion by being generous with your time and resources.

Have faith.

- Be Patient.

- Have a financial plan to guide your spending and giving.

- Be Content. Forsake the love for money (Hebrews 13:5).

- When victimized through greed, allow God to make the crooked path straight.

- Be generous.

- In everything, give thanks.

Chapter 11

Chain of Pride

Pride goes before destruction,
and a haughty spirit before a fall
Proverbs 16:18 (ESV).

The Bible defines pride as arrogance, haughtiness, conceit, and it is listed first in the list of deadly sins. Emphasizing our self over others, and rejecting God's greatness are fundamental characteristics of pride. All of us are proud of something we have accomplished, our family, jobs, awards, completion of a project, etc. A feeling of satisfaction over the completion of a major project, success of a group of people you are leading, or even an award you have received are perfectly normal and I do not think this is the pride referred to here. There are other times we are in situations that we are possibly at fault and have to, as the saying goes, "swallow our pride", admit our mistakes and move on. Here again, this is a normal situation in life that if we respond appropriately at the beginning, it does not lead to a chain of pride that leads to destruction.

It is when we think we are something or did something on our own for recognition that we set ourselves up for a fall. Additionally, being too proud to admit we made a mistake or acting like we know something that we do not know is being prideful. We can become so puffed up about ourselves that our attitude becomes arrogant. In time it negatively impacts our testimony and ability to relate to people we need to help. The fact is that we all came from dirt. Before God did his marvelous work at creation, we were just dirt. His mighty hand made us in the beginning, and we are still nothing without him today.

I heard it said, that people who think they are riding on a high horse, are actually riding on a donkey. Sooner or later a prideful, haughty spirit makes us look foolish. It would be quite embarrassing to show up at the Kentucky Derby thinking we are riding on a high horse, but are actually on donkey. Proverbs 26:12 declares that a man who is wise in his own eyes will not go unpunished. In the case of David, 1 Chronicles 21 reports that he was incited by Satan to count the number of people in his kingdom. This prideful act brought serious punishment upon the people. Another good example of individuals who were puffed up about themselves is found in Matthew Chapter 23 when Jesus condemns the Pharisees for being show-offs. They wore scriptures on their sleeves and forehead, fancy tassels for everyone to see. Jesus told them they were headed for trouble with their pious attitudes.

None of us are immune from being tempted. Jesus himself was tempted when Satan took him to a very high mountain and showed him all the kingdoms of the world that he would give him if he would fall down and worship him. Jesus rebuked him.

> *"Be gone, Satan! For it is written, You shall worship the Lord your God and him only shall you serve."* Matthew 4:10 (ESV)

The most fatal symptom of pride is failure to humble ourselves to God. Pride is one of the seven things specifically listed that God hates. Satan will surely come to tempt us and we have to respond appropriately as did Jesus.

Tale of Three Kings

An account of two kings is recorded in Daniel Chapters 4 and 5. This provides wonderful insight for us as it describes how each of them faced their temptation and the results of their decisions.

King Nebuchadnezzar.

Nebuchadnezzar was the longest reigning and most powerful monarch of the Neo-Babylonian Empire. His pride compelled him to have a statue built in his image and required the people to bow down to it. He boasted of the great Babylon he had built with his own power. King Nebuchadnezzar was troubled by a dream and sought out Daniel to interpret it for him.

Daniel's interpretation revealed that Nebuchadnezzar would lose his kingdom. Indeed, he did lose his kingdom, his mind, ate grass as oxen, dwelled among wild donkeys, his hair grew like eagles' feathers, and his nails grew like birds' claws. After seven years, he lifted up his eyes to heaven and honored God and then his kingdom and everything was returned to him.

> *Now I, Nebuchadnezzar, praise and extol and*
> *honor the King of Heaven; for all his works are*
> *right and his ways are just; and those that walk*
> *in pride he is able to humble.*
>
> Daniel 4:37 (ESV)

King Belshazzar.

Belshazzar was the son of Nebuchadnezzar. Belshazzar returned to his Father's old ways and brought back the golden vessels. He mocked God and threw a party with items taken from the Jewish temple. They drank wine and praised the gods of gold, and of silver, of brass, of iron, of wood, and of stone. During their time of revelry came forth the fingers of a man's hand and wrote on the wall, over the golden candlestick. The king's countenance changed and he was troubled. Just as his father had done, he sent for Daniel to interpret the writing on the wall. He told Daniel if he would interpret the writings on the wall, he would give him a purple robe, a gold chain, and make him the third in the hierarchy of the land. Daniel said, "Keep your gifts, but I will interpret the writing on the wall." The message written was: MENE, MENE,

TEKEL, and PARSIN. Daniel 5:26-28 reveals the meaning of that message that said, God has numbered the days of your reign and has brought it to an end. You have been weighed on the balances and have not measured up. Your kingdom has been divided and given to the Medes and Persians. Because you knew what happened to your father, you knew better. Now you will lose everything. At Belshazzar's command Daniel was robed in purple and a gold chain placed around his neck. That night Belshazzar was slain. Interestingly enough, Daniel ended up with a gold chain for his honesty and obedience and Belshazzar a chain of death for pride and disobedience.

> *Everyone who is arrogant in heart is an abomination to the Lord; be assured, he will not go unpunished.*
>
> Proverbs 16:5 (ESV)

Manasseh

2 Chronicles 33 records that Manasseh became king when he was 12 years old and reigned in Jerusalem for 55 years. He led the people back to their old ways of worshipping Ba'alim, contrary to the ways of his father, Hezekiah. As a result of Manasseh's actions, the Lord brought the hosts of the Assyrian Army against the people and carried him off in bronze chains to Babylon. Here we see Manasseh's pride and failure to humble himself to God resulted in him being bound with chains. Later he repented and was restored.

And he repaired the altar of the Lord, and sacri-
ficed thereon peace offerings and thank offerings
and commanded Judah to serve the Lord God
of Israel.

2 Chronicles 33:16 (KJV)

Sometimes we can be judged or judge others by the car being driven, the house in which one lives, or the clothes being worn. As a result, we may try to be uppity and live a bit above our means just to show off. This is not pleasing to the Lord. While others look at the outward appearances, God looks at the heart and he hates a prideful, haughty spirit. Rather than trying to be clothed in the newest fashion, or drive the latest car, etc. we should clothe ourselves with humility.

Therefore, as God's chosen people, holy and
dearly loved, clothe yourselves with compassion,
kindness, humility, gentleness and patience.

Colossians 3:12 (NIV)

Several years ago, after Dad passed away, I bought my Mother a car. It was not new, but pretty good at the time. Over the years it aged and she would run over mailboxes, back into trees, hit garbage cans and no telling what else (*I finally took HER keys – not fun!*). When she passed away, I kept the car and drove it from time to time just to keep it running. Even with all of its bumps and bruises, it actually runs great. Every time I drove the car, I reflected on the blessing the car was to her. I had purchased the car for a great price, and it was a blessing to the couple who needed to sell the car at that time. It was very reliable and inexpensive for mom to drive. It continued to be a blessing to me for some time after she passed away. Occasionally, I would notice people looking at me funny when I pulled into a superintendent's meeting beside some really nice cars. I did not take offense because I realized they had no idea what value this car represented to me. I knew the blessing it represented and felt humbled. There were a couple of other benefits I observed while driving this old car. First, I didn't have the chain of worry, because a few more bumps and scratches wouldn't hurt, and secondly, it reduced the temptation of greed because I did not have people coming up to me at the gas station wanting money. I looked like I needed money.

Do nothing out of selfish ambition or vain conceit.
Rather, in humility value others above yourselves.
Philippians 2:3 (NIV)

Job remained humble in his serious trials and understood that everything he possessed, God gave him, and also took it away. Yet he said, "May the name of the Lord be praised" (Job 21:1). In the end, Job was restored 100 fold of everything he lost.

And said, naked came I out of my mother's
womb, and naked shall I return thither: the Lord
gave, and the Lord hath taken away; blessed be
the name of the Lord.
Job 1:21(KJV)

Knowledge abounds in our world today. With access to the internet, information about anything is only seconds away. Additionally, creative ideas have a venue to be shared through social media and other online resources. Millions of books, research papers and articles are published online in addition to printed copies being available. With this tremendous amount of knowledge we can risk losing perspective of who we are and what we know in relation to who God is, and the knowledge of God. 1 Corinthians 8:1-2 warns us about claiming to know something that we actually do not know. We can become puffed up over knowledge that we don't have, but claim to have. I am a big proponent of mental capacity building through reading, studying and stretch learning, but it has to be filtered through our knowledge of God and humbling ourselves to Him.

We should be quick to admit our mistakes to avoid a pretense of being perfect. I have learned the best way to eat crow is FAST! Mistakes are part of the maturing process and everybody already knows when we mess up. We are respected more if we are humble in those situations rather than pretending we know something we do not know. When we pretend to know something we do not know, or to be something on our own, we are adding links to the chain of pride. That will ultimately bring us down.

A positive example of overcoming pride occurred recently when Kathy had an accident that resulted in the need for a very difficult surgery. The doctor, who was originally scheduled for the surgery, called that morning to inform us that she was not comfortable in her ability to successfully perform the needed procedure. She informed us of her decision to refer Kathy's case to a more experienced doctor in that particular field, and she apologized profusely for any inconvenience caused by the last minute change. I expressed to her how much I respected the honesty and boldness she demonstrated in acknowledging her limitations. We agreed that the smartest people in the world are those who know what they don't know and admit it.

Additionally, we can become obsessed with our post on social media to the point that we check how many views and hits we receive dozens of times a day. I love the fact that I can keep up with family and friends and share information of my own, however, it can become a source of pride and a "look at me attitude" that is not healthy. What if I checked in on God's word several times a day, or prayed several times a day to see how many hits he has for me?

In our conversations, are we really listening to the other person, or just waiting for our turn to talk? We should not push ourselves back into the limelight by saying, "Yes, but I..." We have to realize that everything we are and have is because of Him and the blessings on our lives. If we constantly give praise and thanksgiving to Him and acknowledge Him in all of our ways, we will not give place to the chain of pride in our lives.

For if anyone thinks he is something, when he is nothing, he deceives himself.

Galatians 6:3 (ESV)

As previously mentioned, we can often be judged by material things, but we have to realize that we are all poor, even the richest person on Earth is poor compared to the riches of Heaven. 2 Corinthians 8:9 declares that Jesus became poor so we could become rich. He wasn't poor. Jesus had all the provisions he needed. True, he was born in a stable, but not because they could not afford a room. Being poor, in this context, contrasts where he came from, Heaven. If you look at it that way, all of us are poor no matter how much we have, compared to the riches of Heaven. But, we all can become rich, in the heavenly sense, through Christ. Finally, being prideful about the material things we have is a pitfall to avoid.

Pride is not about what possessions we have or what position we hold in life, but it is our reaction to it. If we use our position in life to further the Gospel and benefit others, it is positive. But if we use it to impress others, it is negative and the chain of pride starts to set in. Trying to im*press* others bogs down our ability to *press* on.

> *He has showed you, O man, what is good. And what does the Lord require of you? To act justly and to love mercy and to walk humbly with your God.*

> Micah 6:8 (ESV)

Keys to unlock the Chain of Pride

- Pray for the Lord to snap the chain of pride.

- In all of your ways acknowledge him.

- Realize everything you have, or will have, is because of him.

- Recognize who you are in light of who he is.

- Put others success and recognition above yourself.

- Fill other people's bucket and in due time yours will be filled.

- When God bless you with possessions or position, don't get uppity.

- Readily admit your faults and mistakes.

- Develop an appetite for "crow" when you make mistakes. Learn to eat it fast.

- Clothe yourself with humility and walk humbly with God.

Chapter 12

Chain of Anger

He that is slow to anger is better than the mighty;
And he that ruleth his spirit, than he that takes a city.
Proverbs 16:32 (ASV)

Anger is a strong emotion in our natural being that involves a hostile response to perceived provocation, hurt, threat, or when a person feels their personal boundaries are being violated. None of us are immune to pressures of this life that can push us to the point of anger occasionally. The bigger problem occurs when anger controls us and becomes our normal disposition. When this happens, we have put on the chain of anger.

Ephesians 4:24-26 tells us *Be angry and yet do not let the sun go down on your wrath.* So being angry is not the problem, it is when we let the sun go down and still hold on to anger that it becomes a problem.

*A soft answer turneth away wrath; but a grievous
word stirreth up anger.*

Proverbs 15:1 (ASV)

In the Bible there are notable instances of anger. Moses, the most humble man in all the land, succumbed to anger that resulted in life changing consequences for him. Three notable outburst of anger recorded in the Bible points out God's patience with Moses, but at the same time demonstrates there is a tipping point where God draws the line. First, In Exodus 2:11, Moses lost his cool and killed an Egyptian. Then in Exodus 32:19, he became angry because the people worshiped the golden calf and he threw down the tablets. Thirdly, he smote the rock twice rather than speaking to the rock to give forth water as instructed to by God.

As in the case with Moses, none of us are immune from the emotional release of anger. If we respond to our emotion of anger inappropriately, serious consequences will result. Moses is a good example of how anger can impact our lives and alter what God has planned for us. Moses was a mighty leader and an awesome man of God, but his actions resulted in God not allowing him to enter the promise land. Essentially, he chained himself out of receiving the blessing God had for him. What promises are we missing out on because of our anger?

I have known people who are holding on to anger toward individuals and do not even remember why. The person with whom they are angry does not even know it and are going on with a happy life, but the individual who is angry is the one miserable with a bitter spirit. In this case, the angry person is the one being hurt worse. Proverbs 17:22 declares that *a merry heart doeth good like a medicine, but a bitter spirit drieth up the bones.* So the choice is ours. Do we want to have a merry heart or a bitter spirit and dry bones?

In making the choice of how to respond to our angry emotions, we should remember that our actions have consequences. Proverbs 26:27 warns us that if we roll a rock down the mountain with intent of it destroying our neighbor's house, beware, it will land in our house instead and if we dig a pit for our neighbor to fall in, we are the one who will fall in it. Additionally, when we store up wrath against others, we are storing up wrath against ourselves. Anger left unchecked can lead us to revengeful actions that ultimately cause grief for ourselves. Research has shown that harbored ongoing anger can lead to heart problems and other negative physical effects.

When we are the recipient of angry actions, we should not respond with anger. By doing so, we join the ranks of the angry and will release the results of anger on our own life. Failing to respond appropriately may result in us looking foolish.

> *Do not be quickly provoked in your spirit, for*
> *anger resides in the lap of fools.*
>
> Ecclesiastes 7:9 (NIV)

Having the ability to modulate anger can be a good way to clear the air of tension that may exist in relationships or situations. I have had times when a situation exploded between me and others and we let it all out, as they say. Afterwards, we felt better and moved forward with a positive relationship. Getting an issue out in the open and addressing it, is better than harboring bad feelings that lead to bitterness. Bitterness could lead to an angry disposition and soon we hear the sound of clink. The chain is on!

Anger is a way our body tells us something is not right and that we should do something to change it. We need to be sure our physical, mental, emotional and spiritual dimensions are functioning at high levels and congruently aligned in order to maintain control and good judgment.

Using the technique of building space between a stimulus and our response allows time to engage our head (mental), heart (emotional and spiritual), and gut (physical) brains in the process to determine what the best response should be. Additional benefits to this process are that it allows time for our emotions to subside, allows our whole being to come to bare in the decision rather than just our emotions. Our natural emotional design allows us to unwind from angry feelings in about 20 minutes. During those 20 minutes, we should remain calm and allow our head, heart, and gut brains to weigh in on the situation. If we persist with our anger, we are choosing to be angry and allowing the sun to go down on our wrath. In this state, we risk making bad decisions that will have lingering consequences.

Let's practice!

Think of a situation that resulted in an emotional surge of anger and together we will practice the process of responding through our synergetic state with highly functioning mental, physical, emotional and spiritual capacities.

Spiritual Capacity

Our spiritual capacity should be our first line of defense, but we have to turn our spiritual radar on. If we are developing our spiritual capacity everyday with Bible study and prayer, our environment should not be very conducive for entertaining anger. Our shield of Faith will be ready to block the fiery darts that come our way and our discernment will be keen enough to determine between noise and issues that need our attention. We can avoid becoming angry by listening to the Holy Spirit rather than the noise that comes from the drama around us.

We listen to the Holy Spirit through reading the Bible, prayer and fasting, our pastors and spiritual friends. Often the devotional reading of a particular day will be the exact thing I need for that day, even if I didn't realize it at the time. Other times friends will share something with me that is perfect for what I am facing. Often times, it is a still small voice that causes me to notice things that I need to see and hear.

If we just react to every situation without standing on a firm foundation, we will run to and fro ending up unstable in all we do. James Chapter 1 tells us to ask for wisdom and stand on faith, but do not waiver.

Do not waver, for a person with divided loyalty
is as unsettled as a wave of the sea that is blown

and tossed by the wind. Such people should not
expect to receive anything from the Lord. Their
loyalty is divided between God and the world,
and they are unstable in everything they do.

James 1:6-8 (NLT)

Mental Capacity

Earlier we defined anger as a strong emotion in our natural being that involves a strong hostile response to perceived provocation, hurt, threat, or when a person feels their personal boundaries are being violated. Using our head brain, we have to be wise to the strategy of the enemy, and perceive the provocation appropriately by recognizing that our enemy is the devil. We tend to think that, since our difficulty is coming through individuals or situations that they are the enemy, but they are not; it is the devil working through them whether they realize it or not. Through a mental, head brain choice and a renewing of our mind, we can rebuke him, defuse the anger and give praise to God.

Do not conform to the pattern of this world, but
be transformed by the renewing of your mind.
Then you will be able to test and approve what
God's will is-his good, pleasing and perfect will.

Romans 12:2 (NIV)

Physical Capacity

Fight or flight is one physical defense mechanism response to anger. It is important to have already made the choice to sharpen the effectiveness of our physical, mental, emotional and spiritual dimensions before that rush of circumstances that causes anger to rise up in us. However, having not made the choice in advance leaves us vulnerable to the negative possibilities that can result from anger. We must guard against physical reactions that could cause other problems. As mentioned before, we should take time to allow our synergized physical, mental, emotional and spiritual being to be what responds. If we respond just from a physical perspective, it will likely not be a good response. We should allow for the physical ramifications to be considered, our mental dimension time to analyze the situation, our emotions dimension time to unwind, and our spiritual capacity to come to bare based on biblical principles. A life out of balance will respond with sudden acts of anger that can change our lives forever. The chain that anger brings can bind us for a lifetime through the consequences of our actions during an angry state. Rather than looking to win our fight, be the force that is patient and is steady as a rock. Vengeance is mine saith the Lord.

> *Dearly beloved, avenge not yourselves, but rather give place to wrath: for it is written, Vengeance is mine; I will repay, saith the Lord.*
> Romans 12: 19 (KJV)

Emotional Capacity

Remain calm. One great tool for learning to remain calm is to write in a journal. We said earlier that anger is a mask for fear, and fear is a result of forgetting what God has already done in our past. We should write in our journal daily to record the important events of the day. Sometimes we are dealing with good and bad, but whatever the case, writing it down helps to calm our emotions as we reflect. It is great to occasionally read through our journal to reflect on the past and remember the things we have dealt with and God has seen us through. This activity builds faith to believe that whatever is going on now, will work out this time just as it did in the past.

A hot-tempered person stirs up strife, but he who is slow to anger quiets contention.
Proverbs 15:18 (ESV)

My dear brothers and sisters, take note of this: Everyone should be quick to listen, slow to speak and slow to become angry.
James 1:19 (NIV)

However, all aspects of anger are not negative. At times anger can serve as a motivator to stir up passion over a project, situation, or conflict. One good example is when Jesus ran the money changers out of the temple.

Additionally, it is reassuring to know that even when we mess up in a state of anger, God forgives us and helps us. In the case of Moses, even though he got angry and threw down and broke the tablets, God gave him a redo. God said to Moses that he will make new tablets even though YOU broke the others. When you mess up, don't give up because God can rewrite things in our lives too. God was patient with Moses and he will be patient with us. It is important to note, as mentioned earlier, in the case of Moses, there was a tipping point with God that caused Moses not to be able to enter the Promised Land. In Deuteronomy 32:51-52, God reveals to Moses that he will not be able to enter the Promised Land due to the anger he showed in the incident at the waters of Meribah Kadesh. God allowed him to see the Promised Land, but would not allow him to enter.

God is merciful and patient with us, but if we persist in acts of anger, we will allow the chain of anger to keep us from possessing the land he has planned for us.

Keys to unlock the Chain of Anger

Pray for the Lord to snap the chain of anger.

Keep a synergetic state between your mental, physical, emotional and spiritual capacity.

Prepare mentally, physically, emotionally, spiritually daily to build synergetic capacity.

Build a space between the stimulus and your response.

Filter your perception of things through a highly synergized state of being.

Confront negative feelings and avoid storing them up to fester.

Channel strong emotions toward a positive goal or project.

Don't catch every fiery dart that comes your way. Let them drop.

Chapter 13

Chain of Stress

Trouble and distress have come upon me,
but your commands give me delight.
Psalms 119:143(NIV)

S tress is simply the body's response to changes that create taxing demands. When analyzing the impacts of stress, it is apparent there is a difference between distress which refers to negative stress, and eustress which is a term for positive stress. Changes and the trouble it brings are a natural part of life, but they do not have to evolve into distress. We can rest assured that at some point in our life we will encounter family situations, financial issues, job issues, church issues, and other difficulties, but when the storms of this life come our way, rather than retreat to distress, we need to trust the Prince of Peace. Calming the storm is one of the miracles of Jesus reported in the Gospels (Matthew 8:23-27, Mark 4:35-41, and Luke

8:22-25). Jesus calming the storm should bring encouragement and hope for us as we face the storms of life.

Complaining

One way we create our own stress is by complaining. Not only does complaining create a toxic environment for those around us, but most importantly it brings us down. When we hear ourselves complain and remind ourselves of how bad everything is our body reacts to defend itself from this situation resulting in unhealthy stress. Satan can't read our mind, but he can hear us speak. The Bible tells us to guard our heart, so why would we give Satan the password to our heart by letting him know what is troubling us? Instead of complaining, we should speak praise to God and positive words to ourselves. It is so interesting to hear people complain on Monday morning about everything in their life, after singing "What a Mighty God We Serve" on Sunday. Of course there will be trials and troubles in this life, but our God is greater and we should remind ourselves, and Satan, of this fact as we fall back on what God's word says.

> *Guard your heart above all else, for it deter-*
> *mines the course of your life.*
>
> Proverbs 4:23

Financial Stress

Pressure regarding finances can lead to stress. God's word declares in Philippians 4:19, that he will supply all of our needs according to his riches in glory. While it is true God will supply all of our needs, we have to recognize that he knows what we really need, and how to provide for it. Often we ask for things that are not in his will for our lives and that goes against what he knows we really need. Additionally, he will supply for the need in his way. Why should I stress about where the blessing comes from? It is easy to get stressed when the blessing doesn't come wrapped the way we thought it should or from where we thought it should. We also have to remember that God's blessings come to us through other people, and sometimes, people are not obedient, or just plain miss it. In either case, we should relax and let God's provision work its way out for our good.

> *Do not be anxious about anything, but in every-thing by prayer and supplication with thanks-giving let your requests be made known to God. And the peace of God, which surpasses all understanding, will guard your hearts and your minds in Christ Jesus.*
>
> Philippians 4:6-7 (ESV)

Sometimes the financial blessing is not what comes in, but what doesn't go out. A miracle of provision came to Kathy and me on November 28, 2016. On this day, I realized I had a flat tire on my truck. When I went to have it replaced, to the amazement of the salesperson, she realized the age of the tire and the number of miles it had. As she looked at the record of our purchases, she noted that I had purchased that tire in 2007 with an odometer reading of 82,000 miles. On this day that I was replacing the tire, the truck had 252,000 miles recorded. She called her manager and they were amazed and said that to their knowledge 170,000 miles was a new record. The rest of the story is that much of the time between 2007 and 2016, Kathy and I were serving as Music Directors at Fountain of Life Church in Saraland, Alabama, while living in Ocean Springs, Mississippi. It was a 2 hour round trip several times a week. While the salesperson at the tire store was standing in amazement, Kathy and I were discussing the blessing of the difference we could have spent on tires versus the amount we actually spent. We decided the miles we were driving to church did not count toward the wear and tear of the tire. Instead, we were riding on the cloud of Glory. It wouldn't be the first time, because the Israelites' shoes never wore out during their 40 year journey. And, yes we did give God the glory.

But my God shall supply all your need according to his riches in glory by Christ Jesus.
Philippians 4:19 (KJV)

We need to have a financial plan that is developed by both spouses. Our plans should include, paying our bills, not over extending yourself, being generous and by all means, paying tithes. Additionally, we should always seek wisdom from God in making financial decisions.

> *For where your treasure is, there will your heart be also.*
>
> Matthew 6:21 (KJV)

Family Stress

The greatest blessing we have in our lives is our family. Since we care so deeply about them, our love and concern toward them can translate into stress rather quickly. Spouses, children, siblings, parents, grandparents, extended family and even the pet involve working through relationships, hardships, and the cycle of life.

Spousal Stress

Kathy and I got married in 1972, (46 years ago at time of this writing-2019). God has blessed us, but there have been many ups and downs along the way. Even though we have a great deal in common, there are times when we just can't agree on things. In these cases, I tell her I understand we see things differently and appreciate her view. I go on to say that I am sure after a while you will get it right and come around to my way of thinking (only kidding). Seriously, sometimes we just have to know we are not going to agree on things and move on without making a big deal out of it. Additionally, we have found that neither of us should make a major decision without discussing it with each other. As we move forward on that decision, we are in it together. We have decided that we can do and overcome anything, if we work through it together. Knowing that some way, somehow, it is going to be alright diminishes the threat of stress.

Parenting Stress

One of the greatest challenges a family faces is that of raising children. The best scripture we can fall back on is found in Proverbs 22:6.

> *Train up a child in the way he should go: and*
> *when he is old, he will not depart from it.*
>   Proverbs 22:6 (KJV)

As reassuring as this promise is, the word "train" in that scripture is a big one. As parents we often do not know what to do in so many situations as we are raising children and stress comes knocking.

The best thing a parent can do in raising a child in the way they should go is to take them to church, Sunday school, youth service, and church activities. Take advantage of every opportunity to get them connected to the training in the Word. After all, The Word is what we should not "depart" from.

Another stress reliever in parenting is to go ahead and admit that we can't do it by ourselves. We do not have the capacity within ourselves to do it alone. We should utilize the resources at our disposal through school, church, friends, and other people of influence. These resources should not be add-ons, instead they should synergize and work together to send the same message concerning our core values. Besides my parents, Larry McWilliams, my band director in high school, was one of the greatest influences on my life. He was tough on me, and my parents supported him in that process. As a result, I became a band director and continued in the field of education for a 47 year career, and still counting.

Grandparents are another valuable layer of support for children. However, we shouldn't always raise our children the way we were raised. Our natural instincts tend to default to our parents' way of thinking. The truth is they didn't have all of the answers either. As we reflect on our own rearing, we should decide what worked and what didn't work on us. Once we have done that, keep what worked and throw out what didn't.

Parenting is a two way street. Sons and daughters should honor their parents. The Bible is clear on this point. We don't always have to agree with our parents, or even feel the warm fuzzy love, but we must show them the honor and respect God's word declares they are entitled to. Additionally, when we honor our parents, we are modeling how it is done for our children. When we honor our parents not only are we relieving stress, but we are opening a blessings promised to us in the scripture. Proverbs 1:8-9 instructs children to listen to the instruction of their father and mother and it will result in an ornament for their head and a chain around their neck. A chain of honor is far better than a chain of stress.

Occupational Stress

Our work setting consumes a significant amount of our time. In some cases, the amount of time spent at work can be more than time at home with our families. Finding peace and tranquility at work can be a wonderful life experience. The greatest freedom we can have from stress at work comes from not trying to please man, but please God. When we make the decision to honor God in all we do, our desire to impress man diminishes as we cast our cares on God. We will at times feel taken advantage of, betrayed, treated unfairly or discouraged when work relationships get crossways. Sometimes our perception of things in any setting can be influenced by our imagination running wild and blowing things out of proportion. When this happens, we add unnecessary stress to our lives over things that are not even real. Developing a keen sense of perception through our highly functioning mental, physical, emotional and spiritual capacity, gives us a great filter to what we allow in our thoughts.

> *Whatever you do, work at it with all your heart,*
> *as working for the Lord, not for human masters.*
> Colossians 3:23 (NIV)

Sometimes stress comes from people who have authority over us. While it is good to take pride in our work, stressing over it is not good. When stress comes knocking at the door, we should remember we are doing our work as unto the Lord and not allow a state of stress to exist for ourselves. Just press on with what we are supposed to do and let God work things out.

Worry

Worrying is a non-productive waste of time and a significant contributor to stress. As mentioned earlier, many times worry comes from a misguided imagination. When we are stressing over things we can't do anything about, we should start doing something we can do something about. In dealing with stress over things we can't do anything about, we should release them into God's hand. Sometimes those uncomfortable situations are actually God moving on our behalf and it is just the process of his upgrade in our lives. Even if things appear to be going badly, we should have confidence that God will see us through any situation. In the Bible we see that God did some of his best work in the desert and he will do the same for us in our desperate situations.

Dad was an evangelist and I recall one time when we were on our way to Needham, Alabama, where Dad was scheduled to preach. We were traveling a back road in Alabama when the car broke down. We were pretty upset because there was no traffic on this road, and no real way to do anything about our predicament. We prayed that the Lord would help us and God saw our situation. In just a few minutes, out of nowhere, a car pulled up behind us. Dad got out of our car and went back to speak to the driver of the other car. We observed that dad got in the car and after a few minutes, he came back and said everything was going to be alright. He went on to explain that the other car had a telephone and he was able to call for help. My brother and I were young and quite impressed that cars could have a telephone. How could a car have a phone? I realize having a phone would not be a big deal these days, but what are the chances of a car having a phone on a back road in Alabama in the early 1960's? As a result of this, what I believe to be Devine intervention, we made it on time and began a 6 weeks revival and a multitude of people were blessed. To this day, I still encounter people who remember and were blessed in that revival.

In 2 Chronicles 20, a man named Jahaziel, from a long lineage of a Godly family, came out of nowhere to minister to Jehosaphat. Jahaziel is a name in the Hebrew Bible and it means *"God sees"* or "Yah looks." The nation was under a joint attack by the nations of Moab, Ammon, and Edom. Jehoshaphat declared a fast to the Lord and prayed for his help before the assembled nation. *God saw* and used Jahaziel to deliver a Devine message to Jehoshaphat to get him and the inhabitants of Jerusalem moving again. He said, "Give heed, all Judah and the inhabitants of Jerusalem and King Jehoshaphat; thus said the Lord to you, 'Do not fear or be dismayed by this great multitude, for the battle is God's not yours.'" The next morning, Jehoshaphat led his people out, calling them to have faith in the Lord, and leading them in praise. They saw their enemies turn on each other, and won the victory. Judah was at peace thanks to this intervention against its enemies. Likewise, on a back road in Alabama, God sent the Amackers, a Jahaziel that day too because He saw our situation. He sees your situation too and will send a Jahaziel to you as well, if you will give praise, have faith, and press on.

> *If the Lord had not been on our side when people attacked us, they would have swallowed us alive when their anger flared against us; the flood would have engulfed us, the torrent would have swept over us, the raging waters would have swept us away.*
>
> Psalm 124: 2-5 (NIV)

In Matthew 6:26-34, Jesus gives instructions not to worry about our life, food, body and clothes and things of tomorrow. Matthew 6:27 points out that worrying cannot add one day to our lives. If we worry about tomorrow, we will miss what we need to do today. Tomorrow will have its own worries. Worrying and fretting is not pleasing to God. No matter how badly things may appear, God is working behind the scenes for our good.

> *For in the time of trouble he shall hide me in his pavilion: in the secret of his tabernacle shall he hide me; he shall set me up upon a rock.*
>
> Psalms 27:5 (KJV)

Frustration

Frustration can lead to stress and usually comes from trying to do something outside our comfort zone or dealing with unexpected circumstances beyond our control. John Maxwell, in his books on effective leadership, speaks to the notion of sorting out the difference between a problem and a predicament. He points out that problems are the things within our power that we can do something about and predicaments are things and situations we cannot do anything about. We have to treat the two accordingly. Frustration comes when we treat a problem as a predicament and a predicament as a problem. We get frustrated when we try to do something about a predicament, when the best thing to do is ride it out and hang on until it passes. Also we get frustrated when we do nothing about a problem and our inaction makes it a bigger problem. Determining if a situation is a problem or predicament can be a huge stress reliever as we take appropriate action, or non-action.

Feeling frustration over a problem we are trying to solve is actually a positive thing. It is a sign that we are trying to make a difference. If we never try to improve anything, we will not immediately feel frustrated. It takes very little effort to just drift downstream wherever the current takes us. Swimming upstream toward a desired destination is difficult at times. Even though frustration will arise during the journey, it does not compare to the stress that will result from just drifting anywhere that will eventually lead into a worse predicament or problem. When I start to feel frustrated, I step back and analyze where it is coming from. When I realize that it is a result of trying something new, or changing something for the better, it helps me defuse frustration with a positive outlook.

> *Thou wilt keep him in perfect peace, whose mind*
> *is stayed on thee: because he trusteth in thee.*
>
> Isaiah 26:3 (KJV)

Impacts of Stress

Health

Literature is replete with evidence supporting the notion that stress can negatively impact our health. According to an article on forbes.com, the top 7 prescriptions sold are for illnesses related to stress. As they say, an ounce of prevention is better than a pound of cure, so the key is not to allow stress a place in our lives. In other words, never put on the chain of stress.

There is significant evidence that good health practices can reduce or negotiate stress into positive responses and outcomes. In my book, *Power to Press On*, there are specific steps recommended to develop our overall well-being by deliberately doing something every day to build our capacity physically (exercise), mentally (read, stretch learning), emotionally (journal writing) and spiritually (daily devotion). By doing so, we can create a synergetic state of being as all four areas begin functioning at a high level and integrating with each other. I believe living in this synergetic state gives place for eustress to grow in our lives and deters allowing distress in our lives.

Suicide

Among persons aged 15-34, suicide is the second leading cause of death, and the third leading cause among persons aged 10-14. For persons from 35-44 it is fourth leading cause of death. In 2013, suicide was the 10th leading cause of death among all ages. Even though a suicidal state is temporary, most often suicide is premeditated and not impulsive. Some key signs include feelings of hopelessness, perceived burdensomeness, physical health complaints and significant sleep difficulties. Each of these signs can be categorized as a symptom of distress.

In those unfortunate times that I have been affected by incidents of suicide, the occurrence totally surprised me. It has touched me through students, pastors, ministers, fellow church members, friends and relatives. None of us are immune to the attacks against our life that causes contemplation of suicide. We have to realize that everything we say and do impacts our lives as well as those around us. We never know what the tipping point our words and actions may be in those situations. Job's wife, in the midst of his great trials, discouraged him with the admonition to curse God and die (Job 2:9). However, he maintained his trust and hope in God. Like Job, trusting in God is our only hope. The good news is when we trust in God there is always hope.

May the God of hope fill you with all joy and
peace as you trust in him, so that you may over-
flow with hope by the power of the Holy Spirit.

Romans 15:13 (NIV)

No doubt in this life we may feel as if there is not a way of escape from the problems we are facing, but God is faithful and we have to call on his name. 1 Corinthians 10:13 encourages us in knowing that God has already made a way of escape for us. This scripture is in the Bible because God already knew we would come to places of despair because it "is common to man." Because He loves us so much, He wanted us to know there is a way of escape in every situation. We just have to trust Him and pray for him to reveal the emergency exit to us in his way and time.

There hath no temptation taken you but such
as is common to man: but God is faithful, who
will not suffer you to be tempted above that ye
are able; but will with the temptation also make
a way to escape, that ye may be able to bear it.

1 Corinthians 10:13(KJV)

Paul and Silas give us a good example of how to overcome stress. In Acts 16, we see they were beaten, chained and placed in prison. They could have had a real pity party because of the circumstances they were in, but they decided to lift their voice in prayer and praise. As they were singing and giving praise to

God, suddenly there was a great earthquake and their chains were broken. I believe that when we are in the midst of terrible circumstances that can lead to distress, if we will pray and give praise to God, our chains of distress will be broken and we will hear CLINK as the chains fall off.

Keys to unlock the Chain of Stress

- Pray for the Lord to snap the chains of stress.

- Keep your focus on God, not the problem.

- Pray and give praise in the midst of trials.

- Avoid thinking about things too far down the road. Think about the next step.

- Prepare for today and keep showing up.

- Do not procrastinate.

- Have faith that joy comes in the morning.

- Before going to sleep, concentrate on positive things.

- Exercise regularly.

Know that when the enemy comes in like a flood, the Lord will raise a standard against them.

Remember things could be worse.

Write in a journal and reflect on accomplishments of the past.

Relax and let life come to you.

Laugh often.

Breathing exercises and visualization activities can depressurize you in tense moments.

Find a trustworthy friend to confide in when facing difficult challenges and seek professional and spiritual help.

Chapter 14

Chain of Doubt

Jesus answered and said unto them, Verily I say unto you,
If ye have faith, and doubt not, ye shall not only do this which
is done to the fig tree, but also if ye shall say unto this
mountain, Be thou removed, and be thou cast into the sea; it
shall be done. And all things, whatsoever ye shall
ask in prayer, believing, ye shall receive.
Matthew 21:21-22 (KJV)

D oubt, if allowed to rule, can paralyze us from accomplishing our purpose in life and cause us to fall short of what God desires to do for us and through us. When it comes time to step out and do something that we feel the unction to do, doubt will most assuredly flare up. Many times in my own life I allowed doubt to get the best of me and did not move forward with what I felt I should do. Oh how I ended up regretting it. On the other hand, I have jumped on in and felt so rewarded by the result.

Henry Ford said, "Whether you think you can, or you think you can't, you are right." We can readily conjure up a plethora of reasons to doubt ourselves when embarking on a new endeavor or facing an uncertain situation. We can disqualify our self by thinking I am too old. I am too young. I am not the right physical stature. I do not look good. I have been too bad in my past. The list could go on and on. I can honestly say that every new job or endeavor I have started during my career, anxiety and doubt about my ability arises. I believe as we move forward in God's will, there will be anxiety. But if we follow in faith as He leads, it will all work out. It has been said, "If God brings you to it, He will lead you through it."

A study of 300 famous leaders revealed that most of them such as Franklin Roosevelt, Winston Churchill, Albert Einstein and others revealed that 25% of them had handicaps and 75% were born in poverty, came from broken homes, or other troublesome situations. Obviously, these situations could lead to doubting themselves, but it was overcome. Think of what might have happened, or not happened, if these individuals' purpose had not been fulfilled.

All of us have a purpose in life, but we can be faced with doubt in our abilities and fear of failure. It is understandable to hesitate due to temporarily being faced with doubt, but not permanently stopped by putting the chain of doubt on ourselves. God desires to use us and our own uniqueness, knowing that we can fill a need where we are, with what we are, better than anyone else. For example, God used Ehud's left handedness to execute a specific purpose. Judges Chapter 3 reveals that Ehud was left handed allowing him to hide his sword on his right thigh and avoid it being noticed because typically the sword would be on the left thigh. As a result, he was able to "deliver a message" from God to King Eglon with the use of that sword.

There are other notable instances of God using people in unique situations. Naomi was beautiful and was able to change the course of history for her people. A group of lepers, isolated outside the city, were able to warn of an impending attack. Moses stuttered, but was a mighty leader. Abraham, Samuel, and Timothy were used mightily despite their age. Samson, despite his past failures, was used mightily at the end of his life.

As superintendent of education, I enjoy being able to routinely visit schools throughout the district. One day when I was visiting a school, I noticed down one hallway that teachers had created a huge banner with pictures of their student's faces inserted in a cutout of just about every occupational representation you could imagine. In this activity, students were able to choose the profession that they wanted to pursue and have their picture placed in that particular model. I was taking my time enjoying their cute little faces pictured in the display and a little girl came up to me and said, "That is me," as she pointed to her picture.

I said, "I see that" and before I could finish she said, "That is an astronaut, and I am going to be an astronaut."

"Yes you are," I said as she skipped along her merry way leaving me and herself convinced that she was going to be an astronaut. Likewise, God has a purpose for all of our lives. He has our face inserted into a plan that is cut out ready for us to pursue. We should never disqualify ourselves because of fear and doubt that result in neutering the plan before it even starts.

We have to set goals and dreams that are big, and then move in faith without doubt and fear, knowing God will see us through. Setting goals we can accomplish easily on our own, limits God from being glorified by accomplishing things through us that could not have been done without Him. If we do it on our own, we are glorified. If He does it, He is glorified. Because of doubt, too often we run from big challenges when we should overcome doubt and run toward them.

Kathy and I have a house on the Pascagoula River we use as a getaway place on some weekends. If we are there for just a day we often do not worry with putting our big boat in the water, instead we drop the pedal boat in for convenience and time sake. Even though our intention is to pedal the boat for exercise as well as for enjoyment, we have a little trolling motor on the back all powered up and ready just in case we run out of steam on our own. Additionally, we are confident we can pedal a little further up the river knowing that we have our power back up to keep us going and more importantly, make it home. Having this power source to rely on makes the trip much more enjoyable, relaxing, and stress free because we know there is a power source behind us to see us through.

In the spiritual sense, when we cast our cares on him, we have a source of power we can rely on. We can press on without doubt toward the place we are called, knowing we have the power of the Holy Spirit to back us up. Even when the course gets rough with swift current and a strong head wind, we can press on doubt free.

It is impossible to please God without faith. It is not that God says, "Yippee they have faith," rather what pleases him is when we use faith to do what he is calling us to do. The thing He is calling us to do requires faith. Faith makes achieving our goals possible, not easy. We have to open the world of "possible" by realizing that all things are possible through Christ. The word impossible looked at differently can say, *"I'm possible."* No matter how bleak circumstances are, don't give up. Think about it, in the next 5 seconds ANYTHING can happen.

In a split second, an angel came bursting through to deliver Peter moments before Herod was going to have him executed. Peter was bound with two chains and the angel poked him and said, "Get up quickly." And the chains fell off. As they were walking out of the prison, Peter had doubt that this was actually happening and wondered if he was dreaming. When he came to himself, he said, "Now I am sure that the Lord has sent his angel and rescued me from the hand of Herod."

> *Arise up quickly. And the chains fell off from his hands*
>
> Acts 12:7 (KJV).

God is not obligated to reveal his entire plan to us. Since God directs a man's path, why should he worry about the details? It is His plan, however, He does not leave us completely in the dark either. Wisdom and faith help us effectively maneuver through His plan according to His will. We may not realize His plan at the time, but as we move forward, we can look back and see that He has guided us and we didn't even know it.

> A man's steps are from the Lord, how then can man understand his way?
>
> Proverbs 20:24 (ESV)

Man's ways are not God's ways. Doubt can creep into our life when the road we are going down does not make sense to the mainstream way of thinking. We can become discouraged when we are criticized and ridiculed by those around us.

Namaan the leper, for example, came to the prophet Elisha for healing. The prophet instructed him to go down to the Jordan River and dip seven times. Why go to the Jordan River? There are much clearer waters in other nearby rivers and the Jordan River is so muddy. Did he say seven times? Why do I have to dip seven times? With these questions, doubt had an inlet to his way of thinking, but Namaan had to press on and be obedient and dip seven times. Doubt can only be overcome through our action. Namaan could have said, "Nope, this is too stupid, I'm going home." And even after dipping once, twice and three times and there was no healing, it would have been easy to doubt the prophet and stop. However, he pressed on and after the seventh time, he came up with flesh as a little child. If he had not pressed on despite the doubt, he would not have received his healing. In our lives as we face things leading to our blessings that may make no sense to us, we have to trust Him and press on. Just as in the case of Namaan, the blessing will be complete if we follow God's directions. Remember, if the Lord tells us seven times, six won't do!

So can you write a chapter about doubt without including doubting Thomas? No, here it is and it is good news found in John Chapter 20. Thomas had stated unless he could place his fingers into the mark of the nails, or his hands in his side, he would never believe that Jesus was alive. Eight days later, Jesus came to him. Even though Thomas was behind locked doors, shackled with chains of doubt, if you will, Jesus came through the locked doors and stood among them and said, "Peace be with you." Thomas responded with, "My Lord and My God!"

When we are paralyzed with the chains of doubt, Jesus will seek us out as well. He will come through the locked doors and break our chains of doubt and declare, "Peace be with you."

Keys to unlock the Chain of Doubt

Pray for the Lord to snap the chain of doubt.

Strengthen your faith and trust in God by reading the Bible.

Write in a journal and reflect on victories of the past.

Let problems you are facing rejuvenate you. See them as opportunities.

Fall back on what gives you joy.

Let God guide you by moving one direction or the other. He can't guide someone who gives up.

Don't lean on your own understanding. God's way is beyond our comprehension.

If we trust him with our eternal future, can't we trust him with our challenges of today?

Chapter 15

Chain of Discouragement

I, Paul write this greeting in my own hand.
Remember my chains. Grace be with you.
Colossians 4:18 (NIV)

Discouragement is one of the most effective tools Satan uses against us. In fact, 69 times the Bible admonishes us not to become discouraged. All of us are vulnerable to discouragement at times, especially when we begin to move forward with anything worthwhile. Discouragement, unchecked, can cause us to give up, and lose the battle without a fight.

Paul, the writer of most of the New Testament, is an amazing example of someone shackled with discouraging chains. In Colossians chapter 4, three times he refers to his chains and imprisonment. In his final salutation, he asks for prayer and says, "Remember my chains." The Colossians were not only to look to Paul and pray for his release, but also to see the abundant grace and gain inspiration to do all they could for Christ.

The chains of the world can never hold the Word of God down, and we can prove that to the world and to ourselves as we remember the chains that others have used to show that fact.

In 2 Corinthians, Paul summarizes some of the discouraging things that occurred in his ministry. He points out, he was in prison, received 39 stripes five times from the Jews, 3 times beaten with rods, stoned one time, three times shipwrecked, experienced perils of water, perils of robbers, perils from my own countrymen, perils by the brethren, perils in the city, perils in the wilderness, experienced weariness, painfulness, hunger, thirst, fasting, and cold. Yet he declared, *"We are victorious through our Lord Jesus Christ"* and admonishes us *"be ye steadfast, unmoveable, always abounding in the work of the Lord, forasmuch as ye know that your labour is not in vain in the Lord"* (1 Corinthians 15:57-58).

Just as the Apostle Paul needed to be prayed for, at times we too need prayer. Even though as Christians we are on our way to heaven, while here on earth we will surely become bound by this world's shackles occasionally. In these times, it is important to share our needs with our prayer partners rather than keep it all to ourselves. Part of the process of giving it to God is allowing others to intercede for our specific needs.

> *I have told you these things, so that in me you may have peace. In this world you will have trouble, but take heart! I have overcome the world.*
> John 16:33 (NIV)

Discouraging things come our way through many pathways. Sometimes our work situation can be difficult. Other times our family situations and aging parents can begin to drain us. We can become discouraged by worrying too much about other's view of us. We may try to live by pleasing them rather than pursuing our goals and the calling God has on our lives. God may be leading us to a new thing that we are uniquely qualified for, because of what he has already brought us through. We should not become discouraged and disqualify ourselves because others do not think we are good enough. The question should be what does God think about you?

A good example of this is found in 1 Samuel 16, with the selection of David to be King of Israel. Samuel, while being obedient to God, went to Jesse to see his sons in order to choose a king. One by one they were considered, but rejected. Jesse remembered his youngest son and sent for him. When David arrived, God directs Samuel to anoint him as king.

In our lives we have to press on, even when we are discouraged and it looks like others are moving ahead of us. We can be confident, if we are moving in God's will, that our time will come. Sooner or later God will reveal the fact that, "Oh by the way there is Barry (or your name)." If we know our Kingdom purpose in each season we are going through, there is no need to worry or be discouraged. Have full confidence that God is going to bring about everything for our good in His due time.

For I know the plans I have for you, declares
the Lord, plans for welfare and not for evil, to
give you a future and a hope.

Jeremiah 29:11 (ESV)

God can't fulfill his purpose in our lives when we become discouraged and give up. We see in 1 Kings Chapter 19, Elijah got discouraged when Jezebel threatened him and he hid under a juniper tree. An angel came to him twice and *poked* him and said, "Arise and eat." He obeyed and from there he went into a cave discouraged because the children of Israel had forsaken God's covenant and he was alone in pursuing God's will. Jehovah spoke to him and asked, "What are you doing in this cave?" Elijah responded with a summary of all the bad things that had happened, and Jehovah instructed him to come out of the cave and go back the way he came and continue the work. As a result, God preserved a remnant of 7,000 people to continue his work. Another significant result that came from Elijah pressing on was the future anointing of Elisha, who became Elijah's successor and performed twice as many miracles as Elijah did.

In this passage, we see that God pursued Elijah when he was discouraged. Elijah was not calling out to God, but he was sought out to be encouraged by the angel and then Jehovah himself. Likewise, God knows when we are discouraged and will send things our way and poke us to get us moving out from under the juniper tree, and out of the cave, ready to press on. We have to respond like Elijah and get up and get moving. Satan gets nervous when we come out of the cave, under the anointing of the Holy Spirit. He is very content for us to be hiding in a cave, discouraged and useless to the Kingdom.

Two examples of God sending encouragement to me occurred during the campaign of 2015, while I was seeking reelection for my third term as superintendent of the Jackson County School District.

First, one very hot day while going door to door asking for voter support in the upcoming election, I was feeling tired and very discouraged. Suddenly, a gentleman (Ben) pulled up in his car to volunteer to help and in his broken English he said, "It too hot to do by yourself. I help you." He was a hard worker and knocked on over one hundred doors that afternoon. At the end of the day he said, "Let's do tomorrow." Every day for several days he would end by saying, "Let's do tomorrow." Even though he did not speak English extremely well, he could clearly say, "Vote for Barry Amacker" and leave a brochure. There is no telling how much influence he had on the campaign, and it was my happy privilege to recognize him at the victory celebration.

Another encouraging moment in the campaign came after a real discouraging occurrence during the same campaign. I had just left a brochure on the door of a home and as I was leaving, the resident of the home pulled up, looked right at me, tore the brochure in half and threw it in the garbage. That was discouraging!! However, when I returned to my truck, there was a note from another individual on the windshield, accompanied by one of my brochures that read, "Dr. Amacker, you have our support. Please use this brochure you left on our door to give to someone else." Now in isolation this would not have been nearly as meaningful, but the fact that just moments earlier someone had unnecessarily torn up a brochure in my face. It was like the Lord telling me, "I saw that and I have your back, press on."

In discouraging times we have to seek God for strength and encouragement. In Psalm 42:1, the writer uses the imagery of the deer panting for water as an example of how our soul should pant after God. Keep in mind the deer is panting from a position of tiredness and need for refreshment. When we seek after him, he will respond. There have been many encouraging "God Pokes" God has given to me over the years and here are a few worth sharing.

God Poke 1

Before Mom passed away, I was staying with her to take care of her, and sometimes on Sunday mornings I would take a quick break while she was sleeping to go to church. One Sunday I dropped in Oak Park Church of God for a brief time. I arrived just about the time the associate pastor was making the announcements. He stated that they would be having communion at the end of the service. In my heart, I thought, "Oh my I would love to participate in communion," but knew that I would have to leave before the end of the service in order to get back to mother. When the pastor Kip Box, stepped up to give the message, he paused and said, "You know, I am going to change the order of service. I feel like we should do communion right now." I melted. I knew that God had heard my heart cry, and the pastor was being sensitive to the unction from the Holy Spirit and responded in a way that was a tremendous encouragement to me. When we are tired and discouraged, God will minister to us. On the other hand, sometimes we are the ones that need to be sensitive and respond in a way that will encourage others.

God Poke 2

On another occasion, I attempted to go to Oak Park, but upon arriving I couldn't find a parking place (great problem). I went on down the street to another church I know well, Calvary Assembly of God and just as I walked in the door a word was being given that was just for me. The word that was spoken said to "hang on, God sees where you are and He will be with you until you are through it." From this incident, I realized that timing was everything because I could have been at a difference place at a different time, but God had me walking in the right door, at the right place, at the right time, with the right word just for me.

God Poke 3

On another occasion, I was coming out of the grocery store after purchasing food for mom for the week. I was feeling discouraged because the expense of taking care of mom was mounting. In my heart, I wasn't complaining, but I was doubting sustainability in this situation. As you can imagine, 24 hour care was quite expensive on top of our regular family expenses. As I came out of the store, I heard a little guy just preaching from his heart in the parking lot. All he had was a microphone, a speaker, his Bible, and a great deal of boldness. At first, I was only passively listening, but the closer I came to him, his words began to resonate in my heart. It was as if he had heard my inner heart as I wondered about the financial sustainability of this situation. He belted out, "God's word declares, not to worry about your provision. If you give of yourself to help someone, he promises that it will come back to you 100 fold. So don't fret; just keep doing what God has set before you and he will fulfill his promises to you." From that day forward, I never thought about finances again. I just took it day by day, and God provided as he always did throughout Mom and Dad's ministry over the years. I felt badly that I had ever doubted.

> *Hope deferred makes the heart sick, but a desire*
> *fulfilled is a tree of life.*
>
> Proverbs 13:12 (ESV)

God Poke 4

While campaigning door to door in 2015, I had grown accustomed to dealing with dogs. I was barked at, snipped at, and sometimes greeted with a friendly lick. But, one afternoon as I walked down the street knocking on doors, I felt a poke on the back of leg. My first thought was *here we go… another dog.* When I looked back, to my surprise, there was a duck waddling along behind me. This little duck followed me throughout the neighborhood keeping me company, and I would even talk to him every once in a while. When I got to this one particular door, the lady answered the door and looked right past me and said, "You are late for dinner," I turned around and there was the duck behind me. The lady was talking to the duck, but I told her it was not his fault for being late for dinner because he had been helping me campaign. She laughed and said, "Alright then, I will feed him." We laughed and he waddled on in the house, I presume to eat supper.

Over the years when something peculiar happens, I have learned to take the time to reflect on it to see if there is anything God is trying to say, or reveal to me. The duck really did pique my curiosity. So what could He possibly be telling me with this little duck? I thought, *"Surely God was not speaking to me about insurance."*

As I meditated on what this could possibly mean, the notion of a "lame duck" came to mind. An elected official who is not reelected, but has time to complete his/her term is commonly referred to as a lame duck. Since I was running for reelection and if not successful, I would be a lame duck superintendent from august until January. This notion troubled me until the Lord impressed on me that I was not the lame, but Satan is the lame duck. In John 16:11, Jesus reminded His disciples that Satan is the ruler of this world, but he has already been judged. Satan is the ruler of this world, but His day is coming and he is the one that will not be reelected.

As it turned out, the duck was not pointing me to insurance, but assurance. I was reelected to my third term as superintendent in November 2015 for another four year term.

The resounding theme in each of these examples is that a messenger was used. In the Bible there were heavenly messengers and earthly messengers. We can find encouragement all around us, if we are sensitive to what God is trying to say to us, and through us. It is possible that God needs us to be the messenger to encourage or poke someone. He will even poke us with a duck. God will use us with what we have. Ben couldn't speak English very well, but he used what he had. The little preacher in the parking lot had very limited equipment and no support, but he used it boldly. Pastor Kip Box had no knowledge of my inner desire to have communion, but he followed the unction of the Holy Spirit and blessed me. The praise leader at Calvary Assembly did not even know I was there, but followed the urging of the Holy Spirit and gave me a much needed word.

Sometimes we are the one delivering the word of encouragement and other times we are the recipient of encouraging words. In either case, we have to be obedient to the unction of the Holy Spirit and respond. We have to be willing to let others know we are discouraged and be willing to reach out to those we know are discouraged. Paul had the courage to say, in so many words, he was discouraged when he said, "Remember my chains." Jesus also verbalized his discouragement when he asked, "If this bitter cup could pass from him." Be glorified.

> *Saying, Father, if thou be willing, remove this cup from me: nevertheless not my will, but thine, be done.*
>
> Luke 22:42 (KJV)

154

We have to press on through discouraging situations and allow God to be glorified in our lives. In the end, Jesus came through victorious for us when He came back holding the keys to death, hell and the grave. Since He did, we can!!

Keys to unlock the Chain of Discouragement

- Pray for the Lord to snap the chain of discouragement.

- In times of discouragement, fall back on the things that give you joy.

- Stay focused on the goal and the passion of the "why" you are pursuing a particular thing.

- Associate yourself with positive uplifting people.

- Stay away from Mrs. Papoofnic and Mr. Derailit, the notorious misery evangelist.

- Read God's word and discover how heroes in the Bible became discouraged and pressed on to victory.

- Read uplifting books and listen to positive speakers.

- Avoid verbalizing your discouragement. Your words tip the devil off, and start a cycle within your own being of negative feelings.

🔑 Pay attention to God pokes. He will nudge you, if you will pay attention.

🔑 Reflect on victories of the past by looking back in your journal.

🔑 Don't panic, everything is going to be alright.

🔑 Be an encourager.

Final Words

I am He that liveth, and was dead; and behold I am alive for evermore, Amen, and have the keys of hell and of death.
Revelation 1:18 (KJV)

J esus is the ultimate authority regarding our chains. He con-
quered death, hell and the grave. He is the Alpha and Omega,
the beginning and the end. Through Him we can unlock any
chain that we have placed on our lives.

Recently, I had the privilege of hearing Frank DeAngelis
speak, who was the principal at the time of the tragic school
shooting at Columbine High School in 1999. He gave a stir-
ring presentation to superintendents and school leaders in
attendance giving us insight into what is possible and how to
prevent and prepare for such an event in our schools. In one
admonishment, he told us to clearly mark the master key to
the buildings, because in the stress of the moment, your sen-
sory perception goes into shock, preventing you from thinking
clearly on the simplest task. He said that fortunately on that
tragic day, through God's grace, the master key was the first
one he grabbed out of a bundle of several. As a result, he was
able to save several students from harm.

In the spiritual sense, I believe the same is true for us. When the enemy comes in like a flood, we need to have our master key clearly marked to unlock the chains with which Satan would like to shackle us. Jesus Christ is our master key to every chain Satan would like to shackle us with. In the end, however, Revelation chapter 20 points out that Satan is the one who will be bound with chains, so he will not be able to deceive the nations anymore for a thousand years. After 1,000 years, he will be thrown into the fiery lake of burning sulfur, joining the beast and false prophet. There they will be tormented day and night forever and ever.

> *Then I saw an angel coming down from heaven*
> *with the key to bottomless pit and a heavy chain*
> *in his hand. He seized the dragon that was the*
> *old serpent, who is the devil, Satan and bound*
> *him in chains for a 1000 years.*
>
> Revelation 20:1 (NLT)

> *Then the devil, who had deceived them, was*
> *thrown into the fiery lake of burning sulfur,*
> *joining the beast and the false prophet, there they*
> *will be tormented day and night forever and ever.*
>
> Revelation 20:10

In a trip to New York City, we had the opportunity to visit the statue of Liberty in the New York Harbor. Upon further investigation, I discovered, lying at the left foot of Lady Liberty, there is a broken chain. Additionally, her left foot is stepping forward and her right foot is a step behind. The broken chain at her left foot symbolizes freedom and democracy. The chain also represents the end of slavery in America. This historical icon not only speaks loudly regarding democracy and freedom, but it also reveals the importance of moving forward. Stepping forward with her left foot shows the intention to move forward. Additionally, the fact that the chain, even though it is set aside, is still visible reminding us of the chains. It is our choice, once the chains are broken, to move forward, or not. It has been said we are not born to win or lose, but we are born to choose.

In the spiritual sense, Romans 6:6 declares that because of Jesus' work on the cross at Calvary, we are no longer slaves to sin. One phrase in the lyrics of the song, "Statue of Liberty" composed by Neil Enloe, says, "As the Statue of Liberty liberates the citizen, so the cross liberates the Soul." We have been set free. In Hebrews 12:1, we are admonished to set aside the weights that so easily beset us and move forward in victory.

> *Therefore, since we are surrounded by so great a cloud of witnesses (who by faith have testi-fied to the truth of God's faithfulness), stripping off every unnecessary weight and sin which so easily and cleverly entangles us, let us run with endurance and active persistence the race that is set before us.*
>
> Hebrews 12:1 (AMP)

He the son has set free, is free indeed. Press on!!

CPSIA information can be obtained
at www.ICGtesting.com
Printed in the USA
FSHW012145200819
61238FS